The Christian
and the
Magistrate

Roles, Responsibilities,
and Jurisdictions

Further Titles Available from Psalm 78 Ministries

Biblical Greek for Children

Biblical Hebrew for Children

Boundless in His Power: A History of God's working in Jamestown, as told by those who founded it

Driven to Resistance: A History of the Revolutionary War, as told by those who lived it

In Him Will I Trust: A Boy's Account of his Captivity among the American Indians

John Paton for Young Folks

Letters of Comfort to the Persecuted Church

The New England Primer: Essential Textbook of Christian Education

New Testament Greek for the Beginner

Pierre Viret: the Angel of the Reformation

Pirates, Puritans, and the Perils of the High Seas

Without a Home or Country: A Gallant Tale of the Last Stand of the Confederate Navy

For a full listing of available titles, please visit:
www.psalm78ministries.com

The Christian and the Magistrate

Roles, Responsibilities, and Jurisdictions

Pierre Viret

Translated by R. A. Sheats

Psalm 78 Ministries

www.psalm78ministries.com

The Christian and the Magistrate

by Pierre Viret

Translated by R. A. Sheats

Copyright © 2015 R. A. Sheats

All rights reserved.
No part of this publication may be reproduced or distributed in any form or by any means, without written consent from the publisher.

First printing, 2015

Published by:

Psalm 78 Ministries
P. O. Box 950
Monticello, FL 32345

www.psalm78ministries.com

ISBN: 978-1-938822-53-7

Printed in the United States of America.

Biblical quotations are taken from the King James Version of the Holy Scriptures. Divine pronouns have been capitalized.

Table of Contents

Translator's Note 7

1 How Should Man be Governed? 9

2 Warning Against Insurrection and Rebellion 23

3 Christians the Best of Subjects 33

4 Honoring Those in Authority Over Us 37

5 The Ministry of the Magistrates 59

6 The Magistrate's Role Under God 69

7 Jurisdictions and Callings Ordained by God 79

8 Using the Magistrate for Good 91

9 When Can Christians Wage War? 97

10 True Obedience to Magistrates: Examples from Scripture . 109

11 A Christian's Duty Under Ungodly Rulers 123

12 A Note on Sources 129

Translator's Note

The Christian and the Magistrate is a collection of various writings of the Swiss Reformer Pierre Viret which deal with the office of the civil magistrate and the Christian's duty toward those in authority.

As a pastor Viret lived a turbulent life, with many dealings with political and military authorities, both Roman Catholic and Protestant. As a young pastor laboring in Geneva and the surrounding area in the 1530's, he found himself caught up in the battles between the Bernese armies and those of Charles, the duke of Savoy, in the war over Geneva and the Pays de Vaud. While the war was still raging he entered the city of Lausanne, a Catholic stronghold, and labored among Catholic civil authorities as well as Protestant soldiers.

After the Pays de Vaud was won by Bern, the Bernese magistrates held a disputation in Lausanne in 1536 in which various articles of the Christian Faith were to be discussed between Roman Catholics and Reformers. Twenty-five-year-old Viret was chosen to defend the Biblical position on civil magistrates. His defense appears in chapter five of this volume, and is the first recorded statement of Viret's views on civil government.

Viret spent two decades under Bernese authority as a pastor of Lausanne, during which time he had much interaction with the Protestant civil magistrates in an attempt to recover the jurisdictional bounds of the church (which had been usurped by the civil authorities).

In his later years Viret traveled to France for his health,

arriving shortly before the country erupted in civil war. He spent much time in Lyon while it was besieged by Catholic forces. His godly counsel to the civil and military authorities within the city greatly assisted in maintaining order in Lyon, and also resulted in saving the lives of thousands of noncombatants.

After leaving France in 1565, Viret journeyed to Bearn at the invitation of its queen Jeanne d'Albrecht. Soon after settling there another war of religion broke out in which Viret was taken captive by Catholic forces in the city of Pau. He survived his imprisonment and died two years later at the age of sixty.

Writing to Gaspard de Coligny, Viret summed up his feelings of political and military unrest: "By nature I have always loved peace, and was always horrified at all dissensions and troubles." Despite the man's peace-loving nature, God chose to place Viret in some of the most tumultuous situations imaginable. Through these times of political and military turmoil Viret was compelled to search the Scriptures in an effort to instruct his congregations—as well as countless others asking his advice—on the Biblical response to civil government, war, resistance against authorities, tyrants, etc. The writings contained in this volume are a small sampling of some of the applications Viret offered of the Biblical truths pertaining to magistrates and the Christian's duty to them.

For a full listing of the sources of each chapter, please refer to "A Note on Sources" at the end of this volume. Chapter headings and italicized introductory notes have been added.

— R. A. Sheats

CHAPTER ONE

How Should Man be Governed?

The following chapter is taken from Viret's introduction to his commentary on the Ten Commandments, published in 1564.

In which it is shown that the Law of God alone is the true standard by which all good and just government must be ruled and conformed

Seeing that I have determined to explain the Law of God (which must be taken as the standard of all other laws by which men must be ruled and governed), before entering upon its exposition, I shall take a little time to set forth the great difficulties which are always found in governing men well, and the difficulties in seeking to restrain them within the limits of reason, right, and justice, and likewise the reasons for these difficulties. I do this in order to display the only true means to remedy these great evils and to achieve the true union in God which is required in human society, without which men can never exist except in the state which they fear the most—that is, misery and unhappiness in both this world and the next. If this is well known, it can be greatly serviceable to all, in order that all men might hold the Law of God in such value and such esteem as it must be held.

Now, to enter upon this matter, it is fitting firstly to know that there has from time immemorial been a great and very heated debate among wise men regarding the various forms of principalities and governments which have existed from the beginning in states and nations. None have yet been able to give a certain or sure solution to this problem, or one to the contentment of all, because of the great difficulties which are found in all parts. Those who have debated this matter have included all sorts of lordships and public administrations under three types, which they have called after the Greek names, calling the first *monarchy*, the second *aristocracy*, and the third *democracy*.

The first means a form of government and principality in which a single man is the universal head of all those over whom he has charge. This man possesses lordship and sovereign power over all, as the name *monarchy* declares. All kingdoms which have a sovereign king who rules over all others adhere to this form of government.

The second means a principality and a government in which the sovereign lordship is not given to a single man (as a king in his kingdom), nor is it bestowed upon all the people in general (as in a democracy), but to particular persons (and to a fairly large number) who are judged to be the best, the most excellent, and the most fitting to execute this charge, as the name *aristocracy* declares.

The third means a principality and a government in which the sovereign power is not entrusted to a single man, nor even to a certain number of notable persons (as in the two preceding), but is left to all the community in general, who elect by common election those to whom they wish to give the government, though they do this with such a condition that the sovereign power remains in themselves.

If one desired to mix these three forms together, many other varieties could be drawn forth which nevertheless could always be reduced to these three. There would only be a difference in that they could not take simply and purely one of these three uniquely, but several of them, retaining more or less of one or the other.

Now there is indeed much matter here to dispute in order to determine which of these three is the best, the most excellent, the most secure, and the most suitable for the preservation of the nation and human society, and which is the one most to be desired.

Some prefer the first to all the others, and chiefly those who seek to flatter emperors, kings, and other similar monarchs. These allege firstly the example of God as the most perfect that could be, saying that because He is but one God, King, and sovereign Ruler over all creatures, therefore it is required that there be a certain head among men to whom all others are subject.

Another reason these people set forth is that this state of monarchy is not as subject to changes and to factions, intrigues, insurrections, and rebellions as the other two (and particularly democracy). These things are very difficult to avoid where there is a multitude of governors because of the great dissensions and contrary opinions which exist among the diverse sentiments of men, who are so violent and truly difficult to restrain within the limits of reason. Therefore it seems to these people that a ruler who has sovereign power over all can order all his subjects under his obedience much more easily than any other, and can much more easily overcome factions, insurrection, and rebellion, which are true scourges in the common society of mankind. Indeed, of all that can come to pass, they are the most feared.

These same reasons are why even those who prefer the monarchy to the other two also judge aristocracy to be the best after this first one, for it is not as subject to seditions and rebellions because there is not as much government as in the popular state, where many times each tries to be master, and where the most rebellious, seditious, audacious, and the greatest squawkers take the prize.

Thus those also who in no way approve of monarchy because it is so difficult for it to long remain without being transformed into tyranny (as the examples of the ancient histories sufficiently testify), these, I say, choose this second type as the most secure and the best of all, and as the most suitable to take the happy medium which can be taken in a principality and commonwealth, in order that it fall neither to the one side nor to the other, nor approach either of these two extremes which have been set forth—that is, tyranny on the one side and rebellion on the other.

Furthermore, seeing that there are oftentimes great intrigues and factions in this second state, and that it often happens that some are made so great, and are more elevated in such high authority that they subjugate their companions, there are many who therefore prefer the popular state, which is the third option we call democracy. Their reason is that there is less danger of tyranny where there is a greater multitude in whom the sovereign power resides. For some cannot berate the others; and above all, the lower classes are not in so great a danger of being oppressed by the rich than in the second state in which only the most prominent possess the sovereign power. For it seems to them that there is no difference between this second state and the first when they are both converted into tyranny, except that in the first there is only one sovereign tyrant who is superior over all the others, and in the other there are many tyrants who together agree to subjugate all the rest of the people (and all those who seek to resist their tyranny), and who frolic together in the pillaging of the public goods.

What then shall we conclude of all these varieties of opinions, so contrary to each other, and nevertheless all possessing very sensible arguments? When all is well considered and mulled over, we can come to no other conclusion than that men can never be more miserable and so very poorly governed than when they are governed by their fellowmen—that is, by governors who are mortal men as they, no matter what form of government they may take.

For if a single man is the head and holds the sovereign government, either he will be sensible or foolish, wise or stupid, virtuous or wicked. If he is foolish, stupid, and wicked, how great a danger is there when all the people and the whole country depend on such an insane head? For this would be the same as if the government of men were given to a savage beast.

If he is a wise and virtuous man, and one who fears God, there is still a very great danger. The first is that when his reign has reached its end, he may be followed by another who will be wholly contrary to him, and who will destroy all by his tyranny. For, firstly, he is not immortal, as God, but to the contrary he shall certainly die as other men. It may even happen more frequently that the good rulers remain the shortest time in this world, and that they shall be sooner called by God than others, both because the world is not worthy of them, and because God wills by this means to punish men for their sins. Secondly, He does this because He wishes to remove His servants by His mercy in order that they be not corrupted in the midst of the wicked, with whom the whole world is filled. He also does this in order that they not see the evils which must come to pass by the just judgment of God.

We have a very clear example of this, not only in Josiah, but also in others like him who reigned very young in our own times. These God has shown to the world as exquisite pearls among the others, and as the fruit in the bud and in the blossom. And then, having thus given rise to great hopes, He snuffs them out in a moment, as the bud before it comes to the full flower and fruit.

And as to succession, the danger is always greater of worsening than amending, as we still see today before our eyes in many places, just as it also happened to the kingdom of

Judah and of Israel, in which there were precious few good kings. And even those who were the best among them were still very imperfect, and had even fewer good successors. For the majority were great tyrants, enemies of God, and persecutors of the prophets, tearing down all that had been established by their fathers. Now if this happened to the very people who had been chosen by God out of all others and to whom He had given His Law, what hope have we for those who know neither God nor His Word?

Still another danger is that, though the ruler be the greatest and best of men, and the wisest that can be found among all, and though he enjoys a long life, it will nevertheless be very difficult for him to keep himself from being deceived by his counselors and others who are around him, and even those he considers his dearest friends, and in whom he will most confide. For if he is prudent, wise, and virtuous, he will not govern without counsel. But if his counsel is not good and trustworthy, how shall he guard himself against it, as clever, wise, and experienced as he may be, in order that he be not oftentimes deceived? For it is not only difficult, but nearly impossible for one man alone to always guard himself against so many snares, unless it be that he were a little god and not a man. And trustworthy and faithful counsel is something even more difficult to find and to recover than a good and wise ruler.

Therefore it is not wholly without reason that some have raised the question: "Which is more to be feared or desired: an evil ruler with good counsel, or a good ruler with evil counsel?" For if the counsel of the ruler is evil and full of flatterers, ambitious, avaricious, thieves, debauchers, and tyrants (which is fairly standard for courts), the ruler will not govern, but those to whom the ruler and his name serve as a mask shall govern in his name. They shall establish their reign and tyranny by using the ruler just as a decoy serves the huntsmen in their chase, and as idols serve the priests in order to emphasize themselves, and to bring themselves greater advantages by their use. And in this way the tyranny which is to be feared in a monarchy will be converted into what generally occurs in an aristocracy when it is perverted and altered into this tyrannical state which the Greeks call *oligarchy*—that is, a principality of a small number who reign tyrannically and not by true justice, instead of a great number and many people.

As for the next state, the dangers to be found there have already been stated. Although it is easier to prevent tyranny here where many people possess authority than where it is possessed by a single man or a very small number, nevertheless it seldom happens that the majority are the best and overcome the worst, but rather the contrary. And if it happens that the multitude of those who are in authority is greater, the dangers are more to be feared accordingly, and the conspiracies much greater, and the troubles more dangerous.

And among other dangers, there are customarily two great evils which bring great miseries and which often ruin nations. The first is the elections of the magistrates. The second is the judgments and executions of the things ordained by the laws. For where elections devolve upon the community, it is very difficult to have governors and magistrates such as are required; and this happens chiefly for two reasons. The first is a desire which every man has of living in his own carnal liberty and fleshly pleasure without being subject to any laws. This desire is the reason why those to whom the elections belong prefer to have governors and magistrates elected according to their mold and devoted to them, under whom they can live in greater licentiousness, without rebuke or correction, than to have someone who fears God and who shall take them in hand and punish the wrongdoers according to every man's deeds.

The other reason is ambition and greed, which are the reasons why many take the offices of the country by intrigue, either for themselves or for their friends and consorts, and for those by whom they have been corrupted. And this is done not out of a desire to maintain God's honor or the public good or to administer true justice, but is done merely for the honor and earthly profit of those who hope to receive it and to reign above the others.

Seeing that such people who snatch offices and positions by such schemes, and who seek them by such means, do not set forth as their end the glory of God or the edification of His church, or the welfare of the general public, but only their own glory and their own gain, it is not possible that they shall ever fulfill their office and duty as they ought. For, seeing that they depend neither on man nor on God, and that it is in the power of those whom they are to govern to raise them to their position or to abase them, it must necessarily follow that they court and woo all, and that they fear those who ought to fear them, and that they endeavor to gratify and support all those from whom they expect some assistance to advance them, or who they fear shall prevent them from advancing.

One further evil still remains, which is the negligence of judgments and the scorn of good laws and ordinances made for the preservation of the public good. For it often happens that the great alliances and relations which exist in the community prevent the right course of justice, and that the criminals are not brought to justice and punished according to the laws and according to their wrongdoing, but to the contrary they are tolerated.

The chief cause of this proceeds from the fear of the disfavor that those who govern might acquire of such allies who are joined to them if justice were administered as it ought to be, according to the commandment of God, whose Law so often and so expressly forbids having any respect of persons, and commands that just judgment be meted out to all, both to the poor as well as the rich, and to the alien as well as the citizen. Furthermore, it almost always ordinarily happens that within these popular states certain flatterers (who know how to win the good favor of all) are very popular, and easily obtain all they desire. For, seeing that the people are devoted to them, they easily condescend and consent to what pleases them.

Seeing that there are so many drawbacks to all types of civil government, it is not possible that men could ever have justice and live with each other in a lasting peace and remain united unless they possess an authority and a lord who is greater and more excellent in power, wisdom, and goodness than all others combined. God, the Creator of all, shows us this very clearly both in the order which He has established among men and beasts, as well as in the various natures that He has placed within man by joining together the soul and body.

For, firstly, God did not ordain among all the other animals (which are called beasts because of the difference between them and men) some of them to be rulers and lords either over all in general, or over particular species; but He has only given them man as their lord and governor, who differs greatly from the beasts because of the excellent nature within him—particularly the soul, which is of a heavenly and divine nature.

Furthermore, seeing that man is composed of a body and a soul, He has also ordained that the body (which is the lower and baser part, composed of corruptible and earthly matter) be as the servant, subject, and instrument of the soul, which is the nobler part, and of a simpler substance, heavenly and divine, not composed of corruptible elements as the body. Therefore it is quite reasonable that the soul obtains the chief place, and that it commands as ruler, and that the body and all its members are under its command, seeing that they cannot have life, motion, or feeling without it.

Moreover, though the soul, in comparison to the body, is the noblest part of man, nevertheless, just as the head is the chief among all the parts of the body and is as lord of them, so likewise in the soul that part which is called the *spirit* or the *understanding* and *reason* must be taken as the ruler and master, possessing the governance over the other parts, which are the seats of the *will* and the *emotions*. For as man in his body draws nearer to the nature of beasts inasmuch as it is composed of the same matter as they (that is, of corruptible elements), and that in his soul he draws nearer to the nature of God, so also the soul takes more of the earthly nature of the body on the side of the will and the emotions than on the side of the understanding and spirit, which take the highest place. Therefore it is put together somewhat like a little god, to reign over all the rest of himself, both of the soul and body, which is like a little world, just as God reigns in all His created world and governs by His providence in all this great universe of all things, and in all its parts.

Thus, if man desires to reign and govern as he ought, setting before his eyes the example of God, he must not reverse this order we have just discussed. This order is reversed when man gives the rein to his emotions and affections, and takes them as his counselors, and allows them to reign instead of being subject to the understanding, as chambermaids must be subject to their mistress, and as the humble folk to their ruler and king; for the understanding must keep the chief place. For if it is done otherwise, it happens as in a house in which the servants seek to reign over the masters and the children over the parents; and is as a kingdom and lordship in which the subjects rebel and revolt against their lords and governors. Therefore it is not said without cause by certain wise men that, where emotions govern instead of reason, it is as if the horses hitched to a wagon ran away with both the wagon and the driver together, breaking and smashing all, instead of being governed and conducted by the driver.

Therefore wise and prudent men who have known and understood this have very well judged that the understanding and the spirit (which possess the knowledge of things and the judgment to know how to judge as is fitting) must have the rule and the governance in order to hold the will and the emotions under their obedience.

But though this is done, there still remains a great evil. It is that, as excellent as the spirit of man might be, it nevertheless remains enshrouded in a great darkness of error and ignorance because of the natural corruption within him caused by sin. Thus it most often happens that there is nothing within man more contrary to God than his human reason if it be not regenerated by the Spirit of God. This is why his judgment is so corrupted that he cannot discern between good and evil as is required, but to the contrary he judges evil to be good, and good to be evil.

Now the reason must govern, and must be a counsel to itself in order to speak to the will and the emotions (and consequently the whole man), commanding them to follow the good and flee from the evil. But if the mind is so corrupted and so deprived of good counsel that it cannot even direct itself, how can it direct those it must govern?

Furthermore, besides this disadvantage there is also another evil, that where the reason itself sees clearly by the natural light which God has given and by this little glimmer which still remains in it after sin, it nevertheless cannot order the will and emotions to follow its counsel. But to the contrary it must deal with them as a good and wise ruler who seeks to control seditious and rebellious subjects, from whom he can obtain nothing that is just or reasonable.

If man thus encounters so many hindrances within himself (which are the reasons why he cannot and knows not how to even govern himself), how can he ever govern others? Therefore Aristotle did not speak without reason (poor pagan and ignorant of the true God as he was) when he said, "He who entrusts the supreme power to a man entrusts it to a wild beast."[1]

---

[1] Aristotle, *A Treatise on Government*, book III, chapter XVI.

Now we can already judge by what has been said what little hope there is of finding a godly ruler. And even if one could be found, there is still this other evil, that neither legislators nor officers who have the charge to execute what the Law commands, hold the hearts of men in their hands in order to make them willing to obey. None but God, the sovereign Lawgiver, possesses this power. (And what is thus said of the civil government must also be understood of the familial and household government, and of self-government as well.)

For this reason God wished to give the Law Himself to serve as a rule to all men upon earth, to rule their spirit, understanding, will, and emotions, both of those who govern others as well as those who must be governed by them. And He did this in order that all together might acknowledge God alone as their sovereign Ruler and Lord, and acknowledge His servants and ministers, who must all one day give an account before the throne of His majesty. Now He has indeed included in this Law every moral teaching necessary for men to live rightly. And it contains even more—incomparably more—than all the philosophers in all their books, both in their ethics as well as their politics and economics, and than all the legislators who have ever been, and who are still alive, and who shall yet live, in all their laws and ordinances.

Thus, whether we wish to be well instructed in order that we might know how to conduct and govern ourselves in our own persons and individual characters according to right, reason, and justice, or how to govern our households and families, or how to govern in the civil realm, this Law shall supply us with true Christian ethics, politics, and economics, if it be well understood.

Therefore I have labored to explain this holy Law of God as easily and understandably as was possible for me, rather like a sermon, but written in the form of a conversation, which I have followed because it is so useful for instruction.

Now in this exposition I quite amply treat many points which seem to me to be the most necessary for the instruction of men, according to the times in which we find ourselves at present. I do this chiefly in order that all who read this might more easily understand at least a part of the vast treasures of the marvelous wisdom and knowledge of God contained in the few brief words of the Ten Commandments, in order that they might know how to conform their emotions, thoughts, words, works, morals, and all their life in whatever state they may be in, to the rule of the will of God. For this is the sole means of obtaining what we cannot obtain in any other manner whatever, for the reasons which have previously been set forth.

We must not hope that any king, ruler, or people shall ever enjoy a lasting prosperity unless God reigns in all and over all, and unless they are governed by Him, as clearly appears by the promises and curses which He added to His Law. For as He alone can give a perfect Law according to which it is fitting that we be governed, He can likewise give appropriate rulers, magistrates, pastors, and ministers to put that Law into effect, and whom He can fashion as instruments suitable to His service. He can also give power to their offices and ministries to order to His obedience those over whom they have charge. For as He gives His Law to make us understand how we have failed, and to recognize our need, He also gives the Holy Spirit by Jesus Christ His Son, who renews our hearts and gives the gifts and graces necessary to accomplish this Law.

If this be done, then there is neither monarchy, aristocracy, democracy, nor any form of civil government whatever, having its foundation in this Law of God, which shall not be suitable to human society and to all nations over which God shall preside.

On the other hand, if this be not done, we can expect nothing but horrible confusion, destruction, desolation, and utmost ruin of all empires, kingdoms, countries, cities, communities, peoples, nations, and commonwealths. We have sufficient examples of this in all the principalities and in all the peoples who have been upon the earth since the beginning of the world, to induce us to believe it.

CHAPTER TWO

Warning Against Insurrection and Rebellion

The following letter was written by Viret to warn believers of the schemes Satan is accustomed to employ against the church in order to render it odious to the civil magistrates. Viret also instructs those Christians who desired to wage war against their enemies without a duly appointed magistrate or civil official recognized by God as a man in authority who possesses the jurisdiction to wage war. As Viret warns his readers, if a lawfully-appointed magistrate is lacking, believers are warring unjustly and unlawfully, and God will not bless their efforts.

Grace and peace from God our Father through Jesus Christ our Lord, and the communion of the Holy Spirit, and the increase of all His gifts and graces.

Dear brethren, as we have a great occasion to rejoice in the Lord and to give Him thanks for the blessing He daily increases and pours out over the holy ministry of His holy Gospel, and particularly among the people who are more pressed under the yoke of the antichrist than any other, so it is more than necessary that those to whom God shows this grace and mercy diligently and carefully take heed lest by their own fault they themselves become a hindrance to the spread of the Gospel which by the grace of God they see progressing so wonderfully. For the greater the fruit is, so much greater shall the enemy of God and His Church envy them. Therefore he will never cease to employ every means in his power to turn all into trouble and disorder.

But above all we must truly beware of the long-used practice which Satan from all time has always endeavored to employ not only to hinder the ministry of all the true ministers of the Lord—indeed, even of the Son of God Himself—but also to wholly overthrow it if he were able:

The crime of treason and sedition has always been greatly abhorred among men, and not without good reason. For there is nothing more contrary to public peace and human society.

Now, though there have never been men upon earth more innocent of such a crime than the true children of God, nevertheless the enemies of the truth have never ceased to level this charge and accusation against them as if they were the most traitorous and seditious people in all the world, to trouble heaven and earth. The Jews said of Jesus Christ, "We found this fellow perverting the nation, and forbidding to give tribute to Caesar" (Luke 23:2). They not only accused Him as if the crime were already proven against Him, but as if they themselves were astonished at the fact. And these very men who falsely accused Jesus Christ not only of the crime of rebellion, treason, and insurrection, but also of all other crimes and sins (of which He was perfectly innocent), themselves demanded that the just and innocent One be crucified, and that the traitor and seditious murderer Barabbas be set free (Matt. 27:20; Mark 15:7-11; Luke 23:18; John 18:40).

Likewise the seditious men who rose up against Paul and Silas his companion in Philippi accused them in this manner: "These men . . . do exceedingly trouble our city, and teach customs which are not lawful for us to receive, neither to observe" (Acts 16:20-21). And afterward, because Jason received and lodged these holy apostles in his house in Thessalonica, their enemies accused him also, declaring,

"These that have turned the world upside down are come hither also; whom Jason hath received: and these all do contrary to the decrees of Caesar" (Acts 17:6-7).

These examples ought to teach us two useful things. The first is that we must not expect anything new or unusual, and we must not be surprised when our adversaries charge us with these same crimes. For if we follow the Son of God we cannot expect to be exempt from the accusations leveled against Him and His faithful servants. Therefore let it suffice us that our conscience renders us a good testimony before God and His church that our enemies lie and falsely accuse us of what they themselves are guilty of. For the time is coming when God will declare who has been traitorous, seditious, and rebellious, and who obedient, peaceable, and meek; that is, either those who chose to obey God rather than men, and rendered Him the obedience they owed Him; or those who were incited against the true servants of God because the true servants of God did not choose to be rebellious against God as they were, but reproved their rebellion against Him.

The second lesson is, seeing that our adversaries are always laboring as much as they can to make us suspected of such crimes in order to place us under the rage of all the kings and rulers of all the peoples of the earth, so much more carefully must we beware of giving them the least occasion in the world by which they might give some color of truth to their calumnies and false accusations. The best means we can take in this matter is, firstly, to render to all rulers, magistrates, and their officials—whether they be believers or unbelievers—the honor and obedience which God requires of us toward them in His Word, in all that we can do without violating our conscience (Rom. 13:1; 1 Pet. 2:11-15).

Also, we do this that we might further the cause of the Gospel by suffering for our enemies, not by making them suffer for us. For it was not without good reason that Jesus Christ said, "My kingdom is not of this world: if My kingdom were of this world, then would My servants fight, that I should not be delivered to the Jews" (John 18:36).

Our Lord Jesus Christ here teaches us a lesson which is very needful for us. He first clearly shows us that His kingdom is of a different nature than all others. For because it is spiritual, the rule and governance of it is also spiritual. Furthermore, as other kingdoms are often conquered by arms, so they must be kept by the same sort of arms as those used to conquer them. But seeing that Jesus Christ's kingdom is spiritual, He requires no arms of His subjects except spiritual ones. For this is a kingdom of peace, whose residents and citizens have peace with God and also with each other, as brothers and children of the same father. And therefore when the prophets prophesied of it, they said that the people who will abide by the obedience of Jesus Christ and His Gospel will so greatly profit in His school that there will no longer be any mention of war among them (Isa. 2:2-4). Therefore they will beat their weapons and swords into farming implements to cultivate the earth.

The prophets desired to say by this that those who previously were enemies will become friends, and that instead of harming one another, they will not content themselves with only working no more harm, but will even seek to assist each other as much as they can. Now the prophets did not say that believers would bring their enemies to such humility and obedience to God by means of their arms and swords, but that this will be done by means of the teaching which proceeds from Zion and Jerusalem and is proclaimed in the house of the God of Jacob, which is the true Church of Jesus Christ (Micah 4:1-3).

The prophets who spoke thus in no way sought to remove the sword and arms from the magistrates to whom God gave the command to bear them in the defense of the good and the chastisement of the wicked (Rom. 13:1). But this duty pertains to none except those to whom God has committed this charge by their lawful calling.

And if the magistrates do not fulfill their duty, but are instead tyrants and persecutors who uphold the cause of the wicked and persecute the children of God, we must leave the vengeance of such tyranny and iniquity to God; which He shall without fail bring in His own time, as we see by experience that He has always done, and that He shatters the strongest men in the midst of their greatest triumphs (Deut. 32:35; Rom. 12:19). For if the father does not fulfill the duty of a father to his child, but instead acts the part of a tyrant and an abusive man, the child must not chastise and punish the father, but must patiently endure the abuse his father shows him, and pray for him, while in the meantime leaving the case between his father and himself in the hands of God. And if it happens that God wills to punish tyrants and their associates by revolutions and other such extraordinary means, He will do what pleases Him.

Concerning ourselves, we must always wait for His calling, and do nothing until we are well assured of it. For just as Jesus Christ did not conquer us and His kingdom by physical arms, so He does not will to maintain or advance it by such arms. You see by experience all that we say. Who has so strongly advanced the Gospel among you and your brethren, who are of the same condition as you, as you see daily advance before your eyes? Was this done by the arms of kings and rulers, or by your own or any other man's? We can indeed say in truth that the Gospel has been advanced by the arms of our enemies, and not by our own. For when they have taken their arms in hand to persecute us, and when we have turned the other cheek and abandoned our bodies and goods to them, God has always turned their arms against themselves, by which they defeat themselves (just like the Midianites) and leave us with the victory (Judges 7:22). For all the victories that the old and the recent martyrs won for the Church of God were not won by any other means than by suffering; and in suffering they were the strongest of all.

On the other hand, consider what profit those who took up physical arms to champion against their enemies received. And without seeking any faraway examples, let us take those of our own time, which we all remember. We do not desire to set forth the examples of the Anabaptists, because they have a wicked cause, and thus they have also upheld it by wicked means. But let us consider the examples of those who have upheld a righteous cause—indeed, the very cause we uphold—whom God delivered to the edge of the sword of their enemies with great shame and damage done to the Word of God, because they took up arms without a lawful and certain calling. For though the arms which were raised against them were unjustly taken up by their adversaries, nevertheless God did not bless it, but cursed the endeavors of those who called themselves believers and yet sought to resist their enemies by similarly unjust arms, by which they were weakened. For seeing that they took them up without a just and lawful calling of God (either ordinary or extraordinary), their endeavor could not be anything but displeasing to God, and cursed by Him, as the outcome sufficiently testified before all.

Seeing then that we have the express Word of God which forbids us from taking up arms and employing human force without a lawful calling, and that the kingdom of Jesus Christ cannot be upheld except by the same spiritual arms by which it was first established (of which the examples of all times render sufficient testimony that it always ends badly for those who seek to advance and sustain it by force and violence, and that the victory always remains with those who follow the counsel and example of Jesus Christ and have battled against their enemies by suffering), therefore beware of warring against the will of God which He has revealed to you in His Word, and of stepping beyond the bounds of your calling in which He has confined you.

We do not write these things to you without reason.

For we have truly heard that there are many found in various places who are not always easily prevented from flying immediately to their arms and trusting in their own physical strength when they are pressed too far or too shamefully treated by their persecutors. But those who proceed this far, and who prefer to follow their own spirit rather than the Spirit of God and the counsel given them by Him, must beware of the danger in which they place not only themselves, but also the entire Church of God. For firstly, instead of advancing the cause of the Gospel, they place the entire building which has already been established to this point by all the ministers and other servants of the Lord (and particularly by those who in such great numbers in our time have shed their blood for the testimony of the truth) in danger of being wholly ruined.

Furthermore, consider what all the enemies of the truth can do, and how many they have put to death since it pleased God to reveal to men in our day the light of His Word. Tyrants have put many to death, if we wish to recall all those who have been sacrificed for Jesus Christ in the past thirty or forty years. But if men seek to advance the Gospel by revolutions, rebellions, and force of arms, there will in one day be a much greater butchery of men without comparison, both of believers and unbelievers, than the persecutors have been able to do to the children of God in thirty or forty years. And the worst of it is that in doing this the Gospel will not be advanced, but greatly reversed; for men will not be drawn to the faith and the knowledge of God by swords and arms. This work is not human, but divine. And therefore we have no sword by which such a work can be accomplished except the sword of the Spirit, which is the Word of God (Eph. 6:17).

Furthermore, if we have the Gospel without a cross and without persecution, we will transform it into a carnal liberty, as we see the fruits of it in many people for whom the Gospel has cost nothing, either of their possessions or their blood. And therefore they take no account of it, and do not even know what it is. They have a gospel which is not the Gospel except in appearance only. Therefore its proclamation serves for nothing but their condemnation because they have despised it and so villainously abused it.

I know well that some will reply to these things that they are quite content to endure all that it pleases God to bring upon them when rulers and magistrates persecute them. But there are many who cannot exercise such patience when they see that such a heap of common rebels will also mix themselves with the persecution, and by rebellion rise up against the children of God, without having any commission as a magistrate. I confess that this is very difficult to bear. But seeing that we are not magistrates any more than the rebels who rise up against us, if they do evil, we must not do evil like them, and must not become rebels. Let us here remember to render good for evil, and to overcome evil with good, and not be overcome with evil (Matt. 5:43-44; Rom. 12:21). Also remember what Jesus Christ said, and let us note it well: "It is impossible but that offences will come: but woe unto him, through whom they come! It were better for him that a millstone were hanged about his neck, and he cast into the sea" (Luke 17:1-2; Matt. 18:6-7). If Jesus Christ declares such a curse upon those who are the cause of offense—indeed, of only offending the littlest person in the world—how much guiltier shall those be who have offended and worked ruin to the entire Church of God?

Therefore beware of all offenses, and of doing anything without the counsel of God, and without being well assured of His will and your calling and duty. Walk in the fear of the Lord, and leave the government to Him, and He will always bless you more and more. Let every man take heed to his office in order that you might not usurp the office of others, to which you were not called by God.

Those whom the Lord has subjected to the higher powers and to the magistrates, let them beware of snatching the sword that the Lord has not given into their hands, but let them content themselves with the station in which God has placed them.

Pray for all rulers and lords, and for all men in authority—indeed, even for your greatest enemies—that the Lord might always increase His graces more and more upon those to whom He has already made them known, and that it might please Him to convert the lives and actions of the tyrants, that the persecutors may become shepherds and nourishers of His Church.

Above all we commend you to the grace of this good God and Father, praying to Him in the name of His Son Jesus Christ that He will guide you in all things by His Holy Spirit, and that He shall increase His blessings in you with each passing day.

CHAPTER THREE

Christians the Best of Subjects

In this excerpt Viret admonishes his readers that Christians ought to be the most loyal subjects a ruler ever has. Drawing from Biblical examples, Viret explains why the true children of God are the best of subjects, as well as why wicked rulers so often despise them.

There is no doubt that rulers are—beyond all compare—much better served by believers who know the Gospel than by any other men. They have no servants who are less likely to betray them than these. For believers would much prefer to die rather than to have even thought of such a cowardly act as to betray their rulers, because they fear God. Therefore they serve their rulers not only out of the fear they bear them, but also, as Paul requires, for conscience' sake (Rom. 13:5). Likewise they do not only serve for the honors and riches they hope to receive from their lords, but out of the love they bear them, and for the public good, and because they know that by faithfully serving their rulers and masters they serve and obey God (Col. 3:22-23).

But why do other courtesans generally follow the courts? Is it not to advance themselves in honors and riches? Thus in doing this they serve themselves much more than the rulers whose servants they declare themselves to be. Therefore what they do is not done out of regard for their rulers, but for themselves. They do not love their rulers as much as they love their feasts and their possessions and fortunes. Therefore when these things change, they will also have a change of heart. And if the need arises, they will be the first to sell their rulers to the highest bidder. This is the cause of so many revolutions and treasons so often committed against rulers, so much so that they do not know whom they can trust.

But if rulers have many Josephs, Daniels, Ezras, Nehemiahs, Mordecais, a Moses, and others like them in their courts, instead of horned beasts, cardinals, bishops, and so many flatterers, deceivers, and parasites who devour them and their poor people, their affairs would prosper much better than they do. The rulers and their people would be much happier. But God does not bestow this grace upon them, for they do not ask it of Him. Therefore it is a very evil sign when we see that rulers and magistrates cannot bear to have such good men in their courts, but instead chase them out, and are served for the most part by none but flatterers, deceivers, and thieves. For we must not doubt that their ruin is drawing near, particularly when they begin to persecute the Gospel, and when they harbor within their castles incendiaries as their counselors who incite them to do this.

They ought to consider well what good fortune Joseph brought to Potiphar and Pharaoh, and Daniel to Nebuchadnezzar. All the wise men and counselors of Egypt and Babylon did not serve or profit these kings and their kingdoms as much as these two servants of God. And indeed rulers ought to meditate well upon what the Scripture says, that "the Lord blessed the Egyptian's house for Joseph's sake" (Gen. 39:5).

Seeing that the Gospel brings such good to rulers, why do they persecute it? They think like Jereboam, Ahaz, or Herod did. Because the majority of them do not reign with a good conscience, and their conscience accuses them because they are tyrants, therefore they fear what they ought not to fear. And therefore they do not know what they do, or what is good for them. They are not afraid when they have just cause for fear. For they do not acknowledge that God gives and takes away kingdoms as it pleases Him, seeing that He is the sovereign Lord of all (Deut. 2:4-5, 8-9, 24, 31-37; 4:39).

Others are served by religion and their own desires, as Jeroboam (1 Kings 12:26-33). This thing is not a little blasphemy. For if we consider the state of many rulers and magistrates, they do not consider which religion is the best or which is most founded upon the Word of God, but only which best serves their purposes and most assists them in achieving their desires and schemes. And therefore, because the pope has great credit and great power, it seems to them that he can offer them the most aid or harm. This is why they seek to remain in his good graces, and are as Ahaz, who had an altar built in the temple at Jerusalem (against the word of God) according to the altar of Damascus, to better win the favor and good graces of the king of Assyria, and to better retain his favor (2 Kings 16:10-13). For he had dealings with him at the time. And therefore he was allied with him and called him his father.

There are others who act like Herod who had James put to death. Because Herod saw that this greatly pleased the Jews, and particularly the priests, religious rulers, and doctors of Jerusalem, he also laid hands on Peter, whom he intended to sacrifice at the hands of his executioners as he had already sacrificed James (Acts 12:1-3). He did not do this out of any zeal he bore for the religion of the Jews, for he paid no heed to this religion or any other. He had no other concern but for his own reign. But he did this to maintain the favor of the Jews, and to remain in their good graces.

Rulers who do this can also prepare themselves to receive the same wages as Jeroboam, Ahaz, Antiochus, Herod, and other similar tyrants, whose morals they follow (1 Kings 14:14-16; Acts 12:21-23). They often feed poor believers to the lice in their prisons, but God is sufficiently powerful enough to feed the tyrants themselves to both worms and vermin, as He did with Antiochus and Herod after their persecutions (2 Macc. 9:7-10).[1]

God also shows this grace to poor believers and poor innocents, that He does not leave them to be eaten and wholly consumed by worms before they die; but He feeds these tyrants to the worms before they are dead (Rev. 6:9-11). He makes them become their own prison and tomb, and though they seek death, they cannot always find it when they desire it (Rev. 9:6). Their Balaams likewise, with their King Balak, can truly take it as assured that they will receive a like payment as Balaam, Balak, and the Moabites their comrades. For the people who took such pleasure in the tyranny of the tyrants, and who aided them in it, will receive the same payment as those with whom they were united. For the same God who judged and punished them, lives still, and is as just and powerful now as He was then.

---

[1] Though Viret cites the Apocrypha, he did not believe these writings to be inspired, but merely employed them for their historical value, just as he quotes Josephus, Aristotle, and others.

CHAPTER FOUR

Honoring Those in Authority Over Us

*T*he following passage is taken from Viret's exposition of the Ten Commandments. It was written as a conversation between two individuals (Daniel and Timothy), in which Daniel is the teacher and Timothy the student. This selection is taken from the exposition of the fifth commandment.

"Honour thy father and thy mother: that thy days may be long upon the land which the Lord thy God giveth thee."
— Exodus 20:12

HOW ALL THOSE WHO HAVE THE CHARGE OF TEACHING AND OF ADMINISTERING JUSTICE ARE INCLUDED UNDER THE NAME OF FATHER AND MOTHER IN THIS COMMANDMENT, AND THE REASONS WHY

DANIEL: You must simply consider, following what we have just said, that all those who have some charge either of our bodies, souls, or the things pertaining to them, must be regarded by us as fathers and mothers.

TIMOTHY: We will find a great many of them, then.

DANIEL: Without doubt we shall. For firstly, we must take as such the pastors and ministers of the church, as those who have the charge of our souls, seeing that these do for us what our fathers and mothers often cannot do. For all have not the knowledge to be able to teach their children what is necessary for them to know, but to the contrary they must also teach themselves as well as their children.

Furthermore, even when ministers have no other regard than to the public peace and order that God has established in His Church, we must nevertheless always honor those whom God has honored by calling them to this charge, and we must reverence them as our fathers and mothers, both for the honor of Him who called them, as well as because they render Him an account of our souls (Heb. 13:17). We can say the same of the teachers, masters, and instructors of schools and places of education, as well as those who instruct us in our youth; as much as they are toward us what our fathers and mothers would be if they knew how to do it.

Likewise kings, rulers, lords, magistrates, and civil officers who have charge of public justice and government are the first and chief persons included in this commandment. For the protection and defense of our persons and goods are committed to them in order that we might serve God in peace and security of spirit and body under their holy protection (Rom. 13:1-5; 1 Tim. 2:1). This is why the pagans themselves have often called their rulers and governors "fathers of the country" and "shepherds of the people."

Also you must note that God has not given His people an imperfect law in which He has omitted anything suitable to such a Lawgiver as He is, as well as to the people over whom He has willed to be Lawgiver. To the contrary, He has given a perfect Law which encompasses and contains all that concerns His glory and the good of mankind. For if He had done otherwise, He would not be a true Lawgiver, nor a true God, perfect in all His works.

Furthermore, none can truly doubt that He has

ordained all legitimate authority, seeing that without this order the human race could not exist or be preserved in its state or in human society, but would instead necessarily be completely dissolved, and would fall into horrible confusion. Seeing that it is so, we cannot doubt that God has given some law regarding the duty which those in authority and those under authority owe to each other.

Now, seeing that other than this commandment there is no other commandment in these two tables of the Law in which God commanded anything concerning the duty of inferiors toward their superiors, it is easy to see that He has willed to encompass all the generality under the type set forth by Him in this commandment, as we have already explained. For if this were not so, not only would the Law of God not be complete—as it must be—but also He would have omitted from it one of the chiefest and most necessary matters of human society.

Furthermore, the teaching of the prophets, Jesus Christ, and the apostles confirms what I say by what they have written of the office of rulers and magistrates, and of all superiors, and of the duty of subjects and inferiors toward them. For they could make no mention of this if God had never ordained or commanded it in His Law, of which they are faithful expositors.

TIMOTHY: You wish then by the reasons you have just set forth to prove that we must consider that we have as many fathers and mothers as there are people who have a charge or authority over us, and that we owe them the honor which is here commanded us.

DANIEL: It is true.

HOW THOSE WHO INSTRUCT US—AND ABOVE ALL IN THE WORD OF GOD—ARE NECESSARY FOR US, AND HOW THEY DESERVE THE HONOR DUE TO FATHERS AND MOTHERS

TIMOTHY: We have great need of all these fathers. For firstly, if the teaching of God is not so well proclaimed that both great and small are all instructed in it as is necessary for every Christian, and if there is no good discipline in the church to preserve all that is of God and to abolish what is contrary to Him, what would become of all offices of the world? For the Word of God is the rule by which all these offices must be ruled. If this be lacking, there would be neither father, mother, nor child, ruler, lord, officer, subject, or man holding any position whatever, who could fulfill the office to which they were called, firstly to God, and then to each other out of love for Him. If this were not done, what would human life be except violence and brutality—indeed, more brutal than what exists among brute beasts? Therefore it is not written without cause: "the priest's lips should keep knowledge, and they should seek the law at his mouth: for he is the messenger of the LORD of hosts" (Mal. 2:7).

HOW IT IS REQUIRED TO HAVE RULERS AND MAGISTRATES, AND TO HONOR THEM AS FATHERS AND MOTHERS

DANIEL: What you say is true. And if it were thus, it would be much better for men if they had been created brute beasts or if they had never been born, instead of being born for no other reason than to dishonor God and to bring evil upon themselves and others. But though God gave men to His Church to instruct and teach both the great and the small of all positions in order that they might be well instructed, nevertheless human nature is so corrupt and perverse that it cannot align itself to the obedience of the Word of God or submit itself to any discipline whatever. Therefore it is also required that we have other fathers who have the authority and power not only to teach and correct by words, admonitions, exhortations, and rebukes, but who also carry the rod in their hand to chasten in body and goods the rebellious who do not heed the teaching of God, when their works deserve it and the public peace and the preservation of the worship and the church of God requires it.

For if there were no such correctors, there would often be none in safety, not even fathers and mothers toward their children, nor the prophets of God. Therefore God has given the authority and power to kings, rulers, and magistrates to provide for the matters which neither fathers, mothers, nor the pastors and ministers of the church, nor all those who have the charge of teaching, can set in order because of the rebellion, wickedness, and perversity of men. Therefore the title which Aristotle gave to the magistrates in defining their office is not only most honorable, but also agrees well with what Moses wrote of them in Deuteronomy, and Paul in the epistle to the Romans.

TIMOTHY: What is this title?

DANIEL: He called them "Guardians of the Law." And because they ought to be guardians and custodians of it, the Lord commands by Moses that the king "shall write him a copy of this law in a book . . . and he shall read therein all the days of his life" (Deut. 17:18-19). Thus we must not think that rulers and magistrates are only like shepherds and herders who have charge of animals and care for their bodies only, but we must understand that they must also have the care of the souls of their subjects inasmuch as the protecting and preservation of the entirety of the Law and of all within the two tables is committed to them, and that they serve to the salvation of men by upholding holy doctrine—the true worship of God—

by their authority and power, and by protecting the righteous and restraining the wicked, according to the charge given them, as Paul testifies (Rom. 13:3-4).

OF THE OTHER OFFICES CONTAINED IN THIS COMMANDMENT UNDER THE NAME OF FATHER AND MOTHER

TIMOTHY: This is also what I had resolved. It also seems to me that we could truly add to the preceding: first, tutors and guardians who are given to children who lack fathers and mothers (inasmuch as they take their place), and secondly all tradesmen, masters, and artisans who have apprentices to whom they teach their trade. For these must be as fathers and mothers, who fulfill this office toward those who are committed to them for this purpose.

DANIEL: We must not only add this, but must also say that the wife must regard her husband as her father inasmuch as he is the head, as the father of the children, and "because she was taken out of Man" (Gen. 2:23). Servants and handmaids ought to regard their masters and mistresses in the same way, and all young people their elders.

THE TESTIMONY OF THE HOLY SCRIPTURES, BY WHICH IS SHOWN HOW THE PASTORS OF THE CHURCH AND THE TRUE MINISTERS OF THE WORD OF GOD MUST BE REGARDED AS FATHERS

TIMOTHY: I agree well with this. But can you now set forth some clear and express passage from the Holy Scriptures to prove all that you have just said?

DANIEL: It will be simple indeed. First, we clearly see that in former times in the church of Israel the disciples of the prophets and their servants were called the *sons* and *children* of the prophets. And these disciples likewise called their masters the prophets *fathers*. Elisha particularly referred to his master Elijah in this way (2 Kings 2:5, 12, 15). Paul likewise calls Timothy "my own son" for the same reason (1 Tim. 1:2; 2 Tim. 1:2). He also said to the Corinthians that though they had many teachers, yet they had no *fathers* like him (1 Cor. 4:15). He furthermore says that "in Christ Jesus I have begotten you through the Gospel," and that, "I have fed you with milk" (1 Cor. 3:2; 4:15). And, writing to the Galatians, he calls them "my little children, of whom I travail in birth," as the mother in labor, "until Christ be formed in you," that is, until they be fully instructed and reformed into the image of Jesus Christ as true children of God (Gal. 4:19). And in writing to the Thessalonians, he says that he dwelt among them "as a nurse cherisheth her children" (1 Thess. 2:7).

John in his epistles likewise calls those to whom he writes "my little children" (1 John 2:1). This is why Paul, when speaking of the ministers of the church who are called *elders* in Holy Scripture, says, "Let the elders that rule well be counted worthy of double honour, especially they who labour in the word and doctrine" (1 Tim. 5:17). We can add to these the men who teach us, inasmuch as they are given us as pastors, just as we have already said, and also the women who teach the young girls.

TIMOTHY: These are sufficient passages concerning those who have charge of our souls and of instructing us.

THE PASSAGES OF SCRIPTURE IN WHICH RULERS, MAGISTRATES, MASTERS, MISTRESSES, AND ELDERS ARE INCLUDED IN THIS COMMANDMENT UNDER THE NAMES FATHER AND MOTHER

DANIEL: Regarding rulers, Scripture testifies that they were also formerly called fathers, as appears in the name Abimelech, which was common to certain kings, and means "my father the king" or "the king my father" (Gen. 20:18; 26:8). And therefore the counselors of kings and rulers are like their fathers, and this name is also attributed to all the people over whom they have charge, as appears when Joseph is called the "father to Pharaoh" (Gen. 45:8).

Likewise the servants of Naaman who accompanied him on the journey he made to Elisha the prophet called him father, as appears by what they say upon seeing his refusal to obey the word of the prophet: "My father, if the prophet had bid thee do some great thing, wouldest thou not have done it?" (2 Kings 5:13). Indeed, the entirety of Scripture is full of such commands: "My son, fear thou the LORD and the king: and meddle not with them that are given to change" (Prov. 24:21); "Fear God. Honour the king" (1 Pet. 2:17); "Let every soul be subject unto the higher powers, . . . not only for wrath, but also for conscience' sake" (Rom. 13:1, 5); "Submit yourselves to every ordinance of man for the Lord's sake: whether it be to the king, as supreme; or unto governors, as unto them that are sent by him for the punishment of evildoers, and for the praise of them that do well" (1 Pet. 2:13-14).

TIMOTHY: These are many testimonies indeed.

DANIEL: You must also note that after Paul spoke so fully of this matter in the epistle to the Romans, he then immediately proceeded to the matter of Christian love. By this we are instructed that if love does not govern us, we will never fulfill our duty toward our superiors as we ought. For pride begets scorn and rebellion. Therefore if it be not driven from us by humility, it will always produce these wicked fruits within us. But humility cannot exist within us if love does not first reign there, which teaches us to humble ourselves and fulfill our duty to all. And therefore the Lord, desiring to give us laws concerning the love that we owe each other out of love for Him, begins by what children owe their father and mother, and all those under authority to those in authority over them, which after God is the foundation of all true love among all. For who can show how it might be better displayed and practiced than in this way?

TIMOTHY: You have answered this matter quite well.

DANIEL: To the rest there are also many commandments, particularly from the epistles of Paul, of the submission, honor, and obedience which servants owe their masters (Eph. 6:5-8; Col. 3:22-25; 1 Tim. 6:1-2; Titus 2:9-10). Concerning elders, the Lord says, "Thou shalt rise up before the hoary head, and honour the face of the old man, and fear thy God: I am the LORD" (Lev. 19:32). We must note these words well, for God declares that he who does not walk according to this commandment does not fear Him. I could digress into many other passages which could be quoted to this purpose regarding the honor and obedience which inferiors owe to their superiors, which must all be included within this commandment.

WHY THE NAME "FATHER" WAS CHOSEN BY GOD INSTEAD OF ANY OTHER, IN ORDER TO COMPREHEND BY IT ALL THE POSITIONS HE WILLED TO INCLUDE IN THIS COMMANDMENT, AND THE NATURAL REBELLION WITHIN MAN

TIMOTHY: I am quite content with those passages you have quoted. Let us come now to the other point to which you have not yet fully responded. Tell me now why God chose the names *father* and *mother* instead of any other when He willed to include all the positions we have just spoken of.

DANIEL: Man by nature possesses a will strongly opposed to all submission. Therefore he does not wish to be subject to anyone, but instead desires to subject all others to himself. God, knowing this pride of heart and haughtiness of spirit, employed the most natural, gentlest, pleasantest, and least undesirable names and titles of superiority of any that exist among men. He did so in order that He might accustom us to the others by this, and that He might teach us by this to more willingly submit ourselves to them. For the law of nature written on our hearts itself admonishes us to the submission and obedience that we owe our fathers and mothers, by whom God brought us into the world and nourished and instructed us. For we see by experience that nature constrains us to submit ourselves to those who have some charge and power over us, and to consider worthy of honor those from whom we receive some great good, and those to whom we see that God has given excellent gifts to aid and assist us. But there are none who are closer to us in such things than our fathers and mothers, who are by nature the first governors we are given by God.

Thus God by His great wisdom in this Law takes the beginning of human society and the persons who have the government of it, for He wills to commend it to us by these persons who according to natural order are the first in this government—that is, our fathers and mothers. Therefore if men refuse to submit themselves to them and to render them their duty, to whom will they willingly offer obedience? And toward whom will they show themselves just and equitable when they work such iniquity against those to whom they are more obliged than any other creature? Does not such an individual deserve to be taken more for a monster of nature than a man? For what nation has ever existed in the world as barbarous and foreign and so far removed from all humanity, to which nature itself has not taught this lesson, without any other instructor?

Therefore even if God had never given any other law than this natural law I just mentioned, this teacher alone would suffice to convict all rebellious persons and all who are disobedient to fathers and mothers (and consequently to their other superiors), of such a loathsome and beastly ingratitude. For whoever refuses the obedience and submission to those to whom it is due by all divine, human, and natural law, himself attempts to remove and abolish all authority ordained by God, and at the same time endeavors to destroy and ruin all human society, and place all mankind in a condition more than savage, and make a slaughterhouse, and reverse all public order and all order of nature. For seeing that the pride of man is so great that every man seeks to dominate all others, and that none wishes to obey or be subject to one another, what will these men and everything else become except a general and universal den of thieves and murderers, and a mass of savage beasts, mixed and mingled one with another?

AUTHORITIES ORDAINED BY GOD ARE ORDAINED FOR THE PROTECTION AND GENERAL PROFIT OF ALL MANKIND, AND THOSE WHO REFUSE TO SUBMIT THEMSELVES TO THEM ARE MORE SAVAGE THAN BRUTE BEASTS

TIMOTHY: We can clearly judge what you say by the disorders that we daily see in the world. For if the rage and fury of men cannot be held in check by all the rulers and magistrates that exist, what would it be like if there were none at all?

DANIEL: And therefore the empires, kingdoms, and lordships, and the emperors, kings, rulers, and magistrates are not without cause compared in the second dream of Nebuchadnezzar and in his second vision to "a tree in the midst of the earth, . . . strong, and the height thereof reached unto heaven, and the sight thereof to the end of all the earth: the leaves thereof were fair, and the fruit thereof much, and in it was meat for all: the beasts of the field had shadow under it, and the fowls of the heaven dwelt in the boughs thereof, and all flesh was fed of it" (Dan. 4:10-12). This vision was given to Nebuchadnezzar in order that we might understand that the emperors, kings, rulers, and magistrates are like shade trees, under whose shadow all ought to enjoy protection and be protected in peace and rest, such that not only men ought to be maintained in their estate; but even the beasts themselves will acknowledge it. And therefore Daniel also told Nebuchadnezzar, "Thou, O king, art a king of kings: for the God of heaven hath given thee a kingdom, power, and strength, and glory. And wheresoever the children of men dwell, the beasts of the field and the fowls of the heaven hath He given into thine hand, and hath made thee ruler over them all" (Dan. 2:37-38).

We also read that the Lord said to Noah and his children after the flood: "the fear of you and the dread of you shall be upon every beast of the earth, and upon every fowl of the air, upon all that moveth upon the earth, and upon all the fishes of the sea; into your hand are they delivered" (Gen. 9:2). Therefore God gave dominion over all the animals to man, as Moses testifies in the history of creation and in the passage I have just quoted, and David likewise (Gen. 1:28-30; Ps. 8:5-9). We see that all the animals remain in the station in which God placed them, and remain subject to the lord to whom God subjected them. Therefore if we do not wish to render honor and obedience to those whom the Lord has set in authority over us, we show that we are more savage than brute beasts, and render ourselves more hostile and unruly than savage beasts themselves, which are still able to be tamed and controlled.

And therefore we must be sent to their school to learn our lesson and to be taught to obey God, seeing that we are rebels of His express commandment when we refuse to honor and obey those to whom He has subjected us. For we have here an express command. Therefore He clearly says in this commandment (as it is given in Deuteronomy), "Honour thy father and thy mother, as the Lord thy God hath commanded thee." Therefore also Paul afterward commanded that "every soul be subject unto the higher powers. For there is no power but of God: the powers that be are ordained of God. Whosoever therefore resisteth the power, resisteth the ordinance of God: and they that resist shall receive to themselves damnation" (Rom. 13:1-2). Thus we see the commandments, warnings, and testimonies of God, which indeed ought to lead us to the submission and obedience of which we speak.

But if besides this we also consider that the magistrates are given us as protectors in order that we might rest beneath the shade of their wings, who protect our lives, bodies, and goods against all, this must still further incite us to render our duty to them, seeing that they are ordained of God, not for our harm, but for our great benefit, as Paul also testifies, saying, "rulers are not a terror to good works, but to the evil. Wilt thou then not be afraid of the power? Do that which is good, and thou shalt have praise of the same: for he is the minister of God to thee for good. But if thou do that which is evil, be afraid; for he beareth not the sword in vain: for he is the minister of God, a revenger to execute wrath upon him that doeth evil. . . . For this cause pay ye tribute also: for they are God's ministers, attending continually upon this very thing" (Rom. 13:3-4, 6).

You can thus understand in what light those who seek to reject the yoke to which God has submitted them must be esteemed among men, particularly a child who is so ungrateful to his father and mother and so prideful and haughty that he will not submit himself to them as he ought.

HOW THOSE WHO HAVE NOT LEARNED TO HONOR THEIR FATHER AND MOTHER WILL NEVER BE SUITABLE FOR ANY

OFFICE WHATEVER; AND HOW WE MUST REGARD GOD IN THOSE WHOM HE REQUIRES US TO HONOR

TIMOTHY: We must not expect any great good from such a person, no matter what position he might ever be in. For whoever has never learned to obey will also never know how to rule well, or how to command justly.

DANIEL: Experience daily shows this. But to the contrary, he who has first learned and accustomed himself to the submission and obedience due his father and mother, will also truly know well how he must obey others. And, after having learned to obey all those to whom he owes obedience, and to honor all whom he must honor, he will also know well how he ought to govern those whose charge is committed to him when he has attained the degree of those whom he previously obeyed.

There is still one point to note on this, which is that God wills to have these names and titles common with all those whom He established in some authority and position. This is why they are called by the name *father* and *lord* (Isa. 63:16; Matt. 6:4; Luke 11:2). Therefore, seeking to declare to His people the duty and office to which He called them, He said, "If then I be a father, where is Mine honour, and if I be a master, where is My fear?" (Mal. 1:6). Thus whenever we hear the name *father* and *lord*, the name *God* ought to immediately come to mind to admonish us that we must consider the men to whom these names are attributed as representatives of God; and that we must not despise them because of their person, but honor God in them, who represents His image to us in them. Those who understand this well, and who take this consideration, will have no difficulty in rendering the honor due to fathers and mothers to all those whom they recognize were given them by God as fathers and mothers. For we must look only to the Lord with whom we deal, and to His command, and not to the persons He has set in authority over us.

For it is not a question of "Why will I be subject to such or such a person? Is he not a man as myself? Am I not worth as much as he? How is he better than I?" It must be enough for us that God is pleased to have him such. And if we cannot understand the reasons why, He is not required to give us an explanation. Therefore we must simply rely on Him, with no further quarreling or struggling. Otherwise we would be just like the man who seeks to overthrow the government of men, and to dispose of matters to our own pleasure and not to His.

Furthermore, we must consider that if God left this matter to our own choice, every man would choose himself, and would consider himself more worthy of governing and commanding than of being governed and commanded. For we are so prideful and such haughty villains that instead of humbling ourselves and showing deference to others, and preferring one another in honor (as we are admonished by Paul to do), to the contrary we each seek to elevate ourselves above the others, and prefer ourselves to all, and seek to be honored by those whom we ought to honor, and seek to be served instead of serving (Rom. 12:3, 10). In this we practice very badly what Jesus Christ exhorted us to do, admonishing us to "become as little children" in humility, simplicity, and modesty (Matt. 18:3).

IN WHAT SENSE THE NAME "HONOR" MUST BE UNDERSTOOD IN THIS COMMANDMENT, AND WHAT IT COMPRISES

TIMOTHY: But seeing that we already know who we must understand by the names of fathers and mothers, and the reason why God preferred to use these names rather than any other in this commandment, let us now speak of the honor which is here commanded.

DANIEL: There are many passages in the laws given by God as appendices and clarifications of these ten commandments by which we can easily understand the things contained in this word *honor*, which ought always to exist as a recompense and reward due to virtue and kindness. Therefore it is called by a word among the Hebrews which means *heaviness*, which excludes all lightness, thoughtlessness, negligence, and contempt; and carries the meaning of reverence, kindness, and an affection which regards father and mother not as companions, but as lords and masters, and which esteems them as much as we ought to esteem our very life, birth, and everything else God has given us by them. But let us hear the testimony of the Scriptures on this point.

For the first, the Lord commands, "he that curseth his father, or his mother, shall surely be put to death" (Ex. 21:17). By this He clearly declares that He does not desire the child to treat his father and mother with contempt or speak unto them reproachfully, but instead hold them in such regard that he bears them a great reverence in his heart. This He explains even more clearly when He says by Solomon: "He that wasteth his father, and chaseth away his mother, is a son that causeth shame, and bringeth reproach" (Prov. 19:26). And in Leviticus, "Ye shall fear every man his mother, and his father" (Lev. 19:3).

Secondly, there is another law in which He not only commands that "he that curseth his father, or his mother, shall surely be put to death," but also "If a man have a stubborn and rebellious son, which will not obey the voice of his father, or the voice of his mother, . . . then shall his father and his mother lay hold on him, and bring him out unto the elders of his city, . . . And all the men of his city shall stone him with stones, that he die: so shalt thou put evil away from among you; and all Israel shall hear, and fear" (Deut. 21:18-21). Again, you can see by this how much God commends obedience by how grievously He punishes disobedience and rebellion; as He also declares by Solomon, saying, "Hearken unto thy father that begat thee, and despise not thy mother when she is old" (Prov. 23:22). This is the second point that the name *honor* contains.

Thirdly, when Jesus Christ rebukes the scribes and Pharisees because by their traditions they hindered children from honoring their fathers and mothers, He clearly declares that this honor which God here commands us requires a true acknowledgement of the goods that the child has received from his father and mother, by which he is induced to provide for them and assist them in all their needs, or otherwise he dishonors them by his ingratitude. For Jesus Christ rebukes the scribes and Pharisees because by their traditions they persuaded children to offer to the temple what they were required to use to provide for their fathers and mothers, and therefore abandoned them in their lack and needs (Matt. 15:5-6; Mark 7:10-13).

Paul likewise used this word honor in this sense when he spoke of the provision for and wages due the ministers of the Gospel: "Let the elders that rule well be counted worthy of double honour, especially they who labour in the word and doctrine" (1 Tim. 5:17). For he expressly places this first to show how believers are required to provide the things which are necessary for their pastors and ministers. There is no doubt that this honor is also what he commanded to Timothy, to "honour widows that are widows indeed" (1 Tim. 5:3).

For he speaks of this honor by which he desires us to honor both ministers and elders who bear responsibility in the church, as well as widows, even when he writes of the provision that believers owe to both of them. And though the pagans did not possess the written Law of God as the people of Israel, but only natural law, nevertheless this natural law taught them so well that they included under the name of *piety* the honor and reverence which children must render to their fathers and mothers, and every man to his fatherland and country.

TIMOTHY: And what does this word *piety* mean?

DANIEL: It is the honor and reverence men owe to God.

TIMOTHY: Then they sought to make fathers, mothers, and country equal to God, and place them all on the same level.

DANIEL: They did not understand it in this way, but by this language they rather sought to show that, since fathers and mothers hold the place of God as His representatives and most nearly approach His position, so it was quite reasonable to honor them with an honor which is similar to the reverence we owe to God, inasmuch as they represent His person, and that God is more honored in this position, and in those who are included in it, than in any other. And, because one's native land is like a common mother to all (both to fathers and to children), after having given the first degree of reverence to God, they gave the second to the fatherland, and the third to fathers and mothers.

TIMOTHY: What you say ought to bring great shame upon Christians today. For how many of them are there who do not even possess as good a judgment and consideration of these things as the pagans!

DANIEL: Experience alone gives us testimony enough.

THE ORDINANCE OF GOD IS THE FIRST AND CHIEF POINT TO BE CONSIDERED IN THIS HONOR

TIMOTHY: What you mentioned previously of the conjunction of the second table with the first ought to greatly serve to incite us to this honor toward those in authority over us which we are now discussing.

DANIEL: Doubtless so. For the first and the chief honor which is here required of us, and the first foundation of it, is the acknowledgment of God as the Author of this order and human society, to which He gave this rule to govern men in order to instruct them to know Him and His wisdom and justice, and to fear His judgment and obey His will. Therefore Paul, as we just mentioned, said, "there is no power but of God: the powers that be are ordained of God. Whosoever therefore resisteth the power, resisteth the ordinance of God: and they that resist shall receive to themselves damnation" (Rom. 13:1-2). And in Daniel, "He changeth the times and the seasons: He removeth kings, and setteth up kings" (Dan. 2:21).

Thus as God ordained the course and movements of the heaven and stars by His wisdom and counsel, and preserves them, so He has also ordained civil orders, not only approving them as legitimate positions and offices, but also preserving them against the fury of Satan, the author of all confusion. Therefore, seeing that it is so, we must diligently note what Paul says, that "ye must needs be subject, not only for wrath, but for conscience' sake," as those who must answer to God, and not to men only (Rom. 13:5).

And therefore, though the number of wicked men is always greater than that of good men, and those who hate justice and righteousness and all good order are more numerous than those who love them, yet we see by experience that God sustains and preserves the office of the magistrates against all opposition in such a way that it can never be abolished or destroyed. For it is always upheld and sustained by the powerful hand of God because it is His ordinance, and He wills that His majesty be represented and displayed in it.

TIMOTHY: I truly agree with what you say concerning the civil state. But concerning the persons who are called to it, we often see them cast down from their thrones and positions.

DANIEL: It is another matter with states than it is with persons. For if those who abuse it are cast down, this should be no surprise. For this is a just judgment of God, who rightly punishes those who commit such an outrage as to abuse His name and authority by exercising tyranny instead of administering justice rightly as they ought. For they show Him an exceedingly great dishonor and a most grievous insult by exalting the devil to reign instead of Him, and by making themselves his ministers instead of being ministers of God their sovereign Ruler who placed them in such a position. But meanwhile the state always remains, and nothing in it changes but the people.

Furthermore, you must also note that God in His wrath often gives us tyrannical kings and rulers (as He warns His people by His prophets), and makes hypocrisy and wickedness reign, and women, children, and effeminate men because of the sins of the people, yet in His mercy He deposes them when it pleases Him to do so (Hosea 13:11; Job 30:12-15; Isa. 3:4, 12; Eccl. 10:16). And therefore it is written, "He looseth the bond of kings, and girdeth their loins with a girdle. He leadeth princes away spoiled, and overthroweth the mighty" (Job 12:18-19).

TIMOTHY: I would readily agree with what you say, except for the fact that I often see not only tyrants cast down and deposed, but also good rulers and righteous magistrates.

DANIEL: There are many things to consider on the point you bring up. Firstly, there are many who may be esteemed good rulers and righteous magistrates, but who are hypocrites before God, as was Saul for a very long time before he was revealed as being wholly wicked.

Secondly, there is never a king, ruler, or magistrate so just, honest, and perfect that he does not commit many offenses against God in his office, who daily deserves to be deposed from his office if God judged him to the fullest of His judgment, as David frankly declared of himself, judging himself unworthy of the kingdom and honor which God gave him if He had been pleased to punish him for his sins (2 Sam. 7:18-20; 1 Chron. 17:15-18).

It also often happens that God takes into account the sins of the fathers and predecessors with those of their children and successors. Therefore we ought not to be surprised if He at times casts down the very rulers who are regarded as the best.

Furthermore, as God gives tyrants to the people as rods and scourges of His anger because of their sins, so for the same reason He often removes good and just rulers and magistrates and other righteous persons because the people are so unworthy of having them (Isa. 3:1; Heb. 11:36-38). We have a very clear example of this in good King Josiah. But though it may be so, the state ordained by God always remains because of the reasons you have already heard.

CHAPTER FIVE

The Ministry of the Magistrates

In October of 1536 a disputation was held in Lausanne, the largest city of the Pays de Vaud (present French Switzerland). The disputation was organized by the Protestant magistrates of Bern, who sought by this means to formally introduce the Reformation into the Pays de Vaud. Reformers and Roman Catholics gathered to discuss ten cardinal points of the Christian Faith. One of those points (the eighth conclusion) dealt with the definition and duty of the civil magistrate.

Viret, twenty-five years old at the time, was assigned the task of offering a Biblical defense of the necessity of the civil magistrate as well as a definition of his role and power. The following is taken from his defense given that day.

The Eighth Conclusion

In which it is recognized that the civil magistrate is ordained solely by God, is necessary for the preservation of the peace and tranquility of the country, and is the one whom God wills and ordains that all obey, as long as he commands nothing against God

In the fifth conclusion we sufficiently dealt with the ministers of the church and how necessary they are. And now by this conclusion we shall set forth the magistrate and his office, how he is ordained by God, and how he is useful and required in His church. These two administrations are so necessary that, just as a man cannot be a man without possessing both a soul and body, so also human community, unity, and society cannot be maintained without these two offices. Therefore God, who is not the author of confusion but of unity and peace, has placed such an order in His church that, just as man is composed of soul and body, so also He has ordained various ministers, some to serve the soul and minister in spiritual things, and others to maintain the body, temporal goods, and civil order (1 Cor. 14:33).

And, though both serve the church and are ministers of God, yet the first are principally called ministers of the church because they exercise the most excellent, useful, and necessary office without which the church could not be a church. The others (civil magistrates), because their office pertains more to civil affairs—those which concern the body and goods rather than the soul and conscience—employ not only the Word to admonish, exhort, rebuke, and correct (as the ministers of the Gospel), but also weapons and the sword to curb the licentiousness and violence of perverse rebels who seek to disobey the Word of God. For they bear not the sword in vain, but God has given it them to protect and defend the righteous, and to punish and condemn the wicked. And this power is so ordained by God that whoever resists it, resists the very ordinance of God and "shall receive to themselves damnation" (Rom. 13:2).

This is why God gave His name to the magistrates in Holy Scripture, calling them "gods" in order that they might have a reminder that, just as they stand in the place of God who gave them the power of death and life, so also they must judge justly, as representing His judgment and righteousness (Ex. 22:28; Ps. 82:1, 6). They must show no regard, favor, hatred, or avarice for any, but look to God alone, the sovereign

Ruler in their midst, who sees the wrong and right and shall recompense to each one according to their judgment, and cast down and ruin them if they employ His name to promote injustice and iniquity (Ps. 82:1-8).

God also bestows His name upon the magistrates to make known to all that whoever seeks to rise against them provokes God to wrath, and that we must honor them as ministers of God and obey them in all that they command according to their office. For if they are good and faithful, so much more must we obey them, and praise God that He has shown us this mercy. If, however, they are unfaithful, harsh, and tyrants, we must also be subject to them as far as possible without violating the Law of God, who has given them to us to exercise the patience of the saints and to humble and chastise us.

For just as God changes kingdoms and gives them to whomever He pleases (Dan. 2:20-21), and casts down and confounds the rulers and tyrants who do not reign according to His Word or recognize Him as their sovereign Ruler (as appears with Pharaoh, Sennacherib, Nebuchadnezzar, and Saul), so He likewise causes hypocrites to reign because of the sins of the people (Ex. 12:29-33; 2 Chron. 32:1-21; Isa. 36:1-37:38; 2 Kings 18:1-19:37; Daniel 4:1-37; 1 Sam. 13:1-14, 15:10-29; Job 34). And instead of good, wise, and just rulers, counselors, prophets, and other good ministers of whom the world is not worthy, He gives children, insane, drunken, and effeminate rulers to reign over us, to torment and afflict us, that by them we might learn to obey and return to Him, the true Lord and Ruler (Heb. 11; Isa. 3:1-12).

And we have no greater remedy than to pray for them to Him by whom "kings reign, and princes decree justice" (Prov. 8:15), who holds the heart of the king in His hand and turns it wherever He wills, that under them we might enjoy a peaceful life and honor Him, as Paul exhorts us (Prov. 21:1; 1 Tim. 2:1-2).

He also clearly testifies that "there is no power but of God, and the powers that be are ordained of God," as is clearly seen throughout the entirety of Holy Scripture, where we read that God ordained Saul to be king over Israel and set forth the rights which would pertain to him, and what would be required of the people (Rom. 13:1; 1 Sam. 8:10-18). But, because he did not follow the word of God, he was rejected (1 Sam. 13:1-14; 15:10-29).

After Saul many others followed, among whom few indeed walked righteously, as David, Solomon, Josiah, Hezekiah, and Jehoshaphat, who still possessed many imperfections. Afterwards, as often as the people became wicked and idolatrous, so much more wicked rulers were given them, who plundered, murdered, and drove them into captivity, just as Moses foretold, as well as Isaiah, who prophesied of the Babylonian captivity (Lev. 26:14-17; Deut. 28). And though Nebuchadnezzar was unfaithful and idolatrous, Jeremiah nevertheless exhorted the people to obey him, and greatly threatened all who would not do so (Jer. 27:1-13, 29:1-7). And though he was the scourge of God's wrath, yet God (who turns both good and evil to His glory) called him His servant, just as Cyrus is also named pastor and anointed because he was chosen by God to deliver His people from the Babylonian captivity, which was a figure of the great captivity of which we are delivered by the great King and Pastor Jesus Christ (Isa. 44:24-28, 45:1).

And Holy Scripture exempts none from this submission, no matter what state or condition he may be in. But, just as good kings and rulers always had prophets with them, and obeyed their instruction and carried out what they commanded by the Word of God, so also the prophets and priests were subject and obedient to the kings in all things that they commanded according to God, as appears in 2 Kings 16:10-16, 23:1-9, 2 Chronicles 8:12-15, 12:9-11, 19:8-11, 29:1-36, and 31:1-13, which passages expressly reveal how the king commands the Levites and priests, who never transgressed his command.

And our Lord Jesus in no way sought to pervert or alter the order which the Father established. But, acknowledging how necessary it was, He approved and confirmed it, commanding us to render "unto Caesar the things which are Caesar's" (Matt. 22:21). He Himself also gave us an example, not only by words, but by deeds when He commanded Peter to pay the tribute and the drachma, "for Me and thee" (Matt. 17:27), which Joseph and the virgin Mary had previously done when they journeyed to Bethlehem to register and pay the census to the emperor (Luke 2:1-5).

Thus Christ in no way sought to confuse the administration of spiritual things with that of carnal and temporal things, or to reign in this world as earthly rulers do, but to the contrary openly testified by word and work that His kingdom is not of this world (John 18:36). He therefore responded to him who asked Him to divide the inheritance with his brother: "Man, who made Me a judge or divider over you?" (Luke 12:13-14). And when the people sought to make Him king, He hid Himself (John 6:14-15). He also did not refuse to be brought before Pilate and answer him, testifying that his power was given him by God even though he was an idolater (John 19:10-11). His apostles and disciples all followed His example, employing rulers and powers as good creatures of God in His honor and glory, as is evident of Paul, who made use of his Roman citizenship to honor the Gospel in Philippi (Acts 16:35-39) and before the commander Lysias, using the men he gave to protect and defend him, appealing to Caesar to evade the fury and violence of his enemies, and to have occasion to preach the Gospel of Jesus at Rome, as Luke records in the trial of Paul, which is contained in Acts, from the twenty-first chapter to the end.

We must also therefore understand that we must in no way tempt God, but must employ the magistrate as a minister of God, and have him serve to His glory, being subject to him according to God. For so He commands that all souls "be subject unto the higher powers," that is, "to every ordinance of man for the Lord's sake: whether it be to the king, as supreme; or unto governors, as unto them that are sent by Him," as Peter declares, commanding us to honor the king and obey his lords, not only the good and just, but also the harsh (1 Pet. 2:13-14; Rom. 13:1-2; Tit. 3:1).

And both these two show the reasons why. If they are unbelievers, we must not conceal our rebellion and wickedness under the guise of Christian liberty, but must obey them in order that the teaching of the Gospel be not blasphemed, and that we give no opportunity to our adversaries, but that "by doing good you may put to silence the ignorance of foolish men" (1 Pet. 2:13-18, 1 Tim. 6:1-5). For the wickedness and unbelief of the ruler can harm us no more than the unbelief of the father harms the child. If the child is believing, he must regard his father as a minister of God, and must honor and obey his commandments according to God. And the father's unbelief can not harm him any more than the unbelief of the husband can harm the faithful wife (1 Cor. 7:13-14).

If the father treats the child fiercely and harshly, he must bear and endure all patiently, leaving all vengeance to God. For the father has greater authority over the child than the child over him, and it is much more reasonable for the child to bear with him than he with the child. If the father does not fulfill his office, it is not lawful for the child to raise his hand against him and chastise him, but he must still serve and honor him as his father until he seeks to compel him to do something God has forbidden. Then he has the word of Jesus, who said: "If any man come to Me, and hate not his father, and mother, . . . he cannot be My disciple" (Luke 14:26), which He also explains, saying that any man who loves these more than Him is not worthy of Him (Matt. 10:37).

Thus, just as a child must obey and be subject to

father and mother—no matter how evil they may be—until they seek to compel him to transgress the commandment of God, so also subjects must obey their ruler, who is the father of the country and shepherd of the people. If he is a tyrant and afflicts the poor people, it is God who will judge between us and him, before whom all names are recorded, to whose knowledge we must leave him, and patiently bear his tyranny until God establishes order as He pleases. During which time we must exercise the means that He provides, without tumult or insurrection.

But if his tyranny seeks to extend itself beyond the body and goods, and he seeks to compel us to commit idolatry and transgress the commandments of God, in such case we must hate him—that is, love God more than him, and obey Him, the supreme Ruler, more readily than men, who are no more than dust and ashes, just as the apostles, who feared Him who can kill the body and the soul more than those who killed Jesus Christ (Acts 5:29).

Daniel also, though he was subject and obedient to the king of Babylon, nevertheless preferred to be cast into the den of lions rather than obey the wicked command of the king and remain only three days without praying to God, as the three young men had already done, choosing to be thrown into the fiery furnace that Nebuchadnezzar had made seven times hotter rather than bow, worship, or adore the great image and statue of gold which he had made—indeed, than to even do anything similar (Dan. 3, 6). And many other good servants of God were killed, knowing that if they sought to please men, they could not be servants of God (Gal. 1:10).

Whoever does otherwise abuses the ordinance of God, ignoring that God has ordained the ruler for the people in good, not the people for the ruler in evil, and has no better excuse before God than Adam, who excused himself because of the woman whom God had given him for a helpmeet and not for sin; or as the citizens of the city of Naboth, who unjustly murdered the just Naboth to please King Ahab and Jezebel the idolatress; or Pilate who, out of fear of the Jews and fear of being deprived of his office, condemned Jesus Christ to death (Gen. 3:12; 1 Kings 21:7-14; John 19:12-16).

Therefore it is exceedingly necessary for us to prudently beware of offending either on one side or the other. We must take care that we do not attribute to the magistrate what does not pertain to him, fearing and honoring him more than God, or that, by rebellion and disobedience, we provoke God against ourselves.

And as it is commanded us to obey tyrants and unbelievers, so much greater reason have we to keep ourselves from despising believing lords because they are brothers and beloved and partakers of the blessing (1 Tim. 6:2). Instead we are indeed constrained to praise God who gives us good and believing rulers, as we ourselves, and we must honor them as fathers, not only out of fear of His wrath, but for conscience' sake, knowing that if we hold back what is their due, we are thieves and act as wickedly as though we stole from our own father. For, seeing that they are ordained by God to serve us as fathers to children, to protect and defend us from injury and violence, to the praise of the good and vengeance of the wicked, so also we are bound to support them.

And it is commanded of us to pay their censuses, tributes, taxes, and other things which are due them, as is fully revealed and declared by Paul (Rom. 13:1-6; 1 Pet. 2:13-17). For this is the honor we owe them—just as the honor that we owe our father and mother is to obey them—and also their ministers who execute their decrees, seeing that the ruler cannot provide for what must be done if he has no one to do it (Matt. 15:3-9).

Therefore, just as the church by the Word of God is instructed and taught that the magistrate is ordained of God and necessary to preserve the peace and tranquility of the country (which the present conclusion maintains), so it also recognizes him as the minister of God, and rejects as false servants of God those who seek to place confusion in the church by denying that we have need of a magistrate, or declaring that he must be Christian. For though in Jesus Christ there is neither male, female, slave, nor free, this concerns the spirit and salvation given us by Jesus Christ, in which there is no difference between man and woman, slave and free, for they are all redeemed at the same price and are members of the body of Jesus (Gal. 3:28). But this in no way removes the difference between man and woman, slave and free, and son and father, with regard to their station and body. Would we not think a man out of his mind who sought to confuse these things, as those poor possessed spirits who are seeking to make a platonic republic and fill all with confusion?

If we were wholly spiritual and the flesh had fully departed from us—which shall not be accomplished until the resurrection—we would have need of neither ruler nor justice. For we ourselves, loving our neighbor and rendering to all their due, would work true justice and would be a law to ourselves. But while we are sinners and the wolves are still mingled among the sheep of Jesus Christ, God, because of our perversity and wickedness, established pastors wielding the sword to defend the sheep, not only to kill and terrify, but to give fear to the wolves and punish the wicked; otherwise the world would be no more than a slaughterhouse, a den of thieves, and a horrible confusion and desolation. Indeed, if this sword were not ordained to correct those who seek to transgress the preaching of the Word of God by a rampant licentiousness and who spoil, trouble, and ruin the good, it would be better to dwell among savage beasts than among men.

When the tax collectors and soldiers came to John, he did not forbid them from serving the ruler to the aid of the country, but taught them how they must fulfill their office without offering injury or wrong to any (Luke 3:12-14).

Likewise, when Philip baptized the eunuch who was treasurer to the king of the Ethiopians, when Peter baptized Cornelius the centurion, and when Paul also preached the Gospel to the proconsul, Paulus Sergius, they did not command them to abandon their positions by saying that unless they did so they could not be Christians (Acts 8:26-38; 10:1-48). Therefore the church cannot approve such seditious and subversive spirits which proceed from the spirit who is the author of trouble, quarrel, and confusion, and thus condemn those who, feigning to be ministers of the church, have overrun and usurped the authority of the sword, attributing to themselves both temporal and spiritual power, by which they do great wrong and injury to the lawful and natural rulers, and show well that they have no share in Jesus Christ or His disciples.

CHAPTER SIX

The Magistrate's Role Under God

*T**he following excerpt is taken from the first volume of Viret's* Instruction Chrestienne en la doctrine de la loi et de l'Evangile, *in which he addresses those who seek to use their allegiance to the civil government to justify their rebellion against God's commands.*

> *Concerning those who disguise their rebellion against the Word and will of God under the excuse of the obedience they owe to the laws made by their rulers contrary to that Word; and those who leave their consciences to the care of their pastors*

TIMOTHY: There are others who seem to have a slightly better excuse, saying that they wish to live as their rulers, and that they are bound to obey their laws and statutes. There are others who say that they rely upon their bishops and priests (who are their spiritual shepherds and fathers) because they have the charge of their souls and consciences and must give an account of them, and because they bear the responsibility for them if they are poorly instructed because of their fault.

DANIEL: I fear that it will happen to many of those who seek such means of escape as it did to the citizens and inhabitants of Jerusalem, who were astonished that their governors and lords permitted Jesus Christ to teach publicly in the temple without contradicting Him, seeing that they had previously attempted to put Him to death. As long as they thought that their governors and pastors condemned Jesus Christ and His teaching, and as long as they forbade anyone to speak to Him, this sufficed to prevent them from living for Him (John 7:25-27).

But after they saw that their lords left off pursuing Him as they had intended, and that it appeared that they had changed their mind and now acknowledged Jesus Christ as the true Messiah, they no longer deferred to the judgment and conscience of their lords and prelates, and no longer followed the opinion they thought they had of Jesus Christ, but instead they justified themselves by their masterful theology, and began to dispute among themselves in order to place an obstacle and a hindrance in their own way, saying, "We know this man whence He is: but when Christ cometh, no man knoweth whence He is" (John 7:27). Why didn't they say, "We must acknowledge Him as the Christ, and follow our pastors"? We see here the nature of men, quick to follow evil examples rather than good.

TIMOTHY: It is true.

DANIEL: Furthermore, I wonder if those who declare they do these things out of the good opinion they have of their rulers, and of seeking so particularly to fulfill their duty and obedience to their laws and ordinances, would have as much conscience to sell and betray them if they had need to and if some good occasion offered itself by which they might better raise themselves in honors toward other rulers than their own. But I would truly like to know if they have as much difficulty in violating the good statutes which are made by their rulers to preserve the public good, and whether—when they can do it secretly and without placing themselves in any danger—they withhold the taxes that are justly due their rulers by the commandment of God. Are they as hesitant to break these laws as they are to transgress the wicked edicts made against all right, to hinder the course of the Gospel, and to inquire into the will of God and the matters necessary for the salvation of their souls, and to serve God as He has commanded in His Law (Rom. 13:1-7; Matt. 22:16-22)?

I greatly fear that this grand obedience of the majority of these toward their rulers and their laws does not proceed from anything but the rebellion against God within their hearts, and not from any good affection they have for their rulers and their statutes, or out of any loyalty existing within them. But because they dare not openly display the wickedness of their heart, they are quite happy to have this excuse, and prefer tyrannical rulers who forbid them from hearing the voice of God rather than Christian rulers who compel them to hear and to serve and honor Him.

THOSE WHO ARE IDOLATERS OF THEIR RULERS, PREFERRING THEIR LAWS TO GOD'S LAWS; AND THE AUTHORITY OF THE WORD OF GOD OVER ALL MEN AND OVER ALL THEIR LAWS

TIMOTHY: I do not doubt that there are many such as these. But there are also many others who are not of such a vile, worldly character, but who are simply idolaters of their rulers.

DANIEL: You rightly call such people idolaters. For because they hold their rulers as their law in matters of religion and conscience, without in any way inquiring into the will of God, they make them into their gods and idols, and do them great wrong. For it does not pertain to a ruler—or to any other creature whatever, no matter what great excellence he may have—nor even to angels themselves, to make laws concerning the religion and worship of God, but only to God alone, to whom this worship pertains, and the honor of such things. Therefore Paul says that "though we, or an angel from heaven, preach any other gospel unto you than that which we have preached unto you," which is the true Gospel of Jesus Christ, "let him be accursed" (Gal. 1:8). If he subjects the angels themselves to the Word of God, have not mortal men even greater reason to be subject to it? For to whom does it pertain to give laws: either to rulers or to subjects?

TIMOTHY: It pertains to rulers to give them, and to subjects to receive and obey them.

DANIEL: Thus, seeing that religion concerns nothing except the honor and worship due to God alone, and seeing that He wills no one to have dominion over the souls and consciences but Himself, and that He has as much lordship over the greatest monarchs, emperors, kings, rulers, and lords as over the least of their subjects, what presumption would it be for them to dare to undertake to give laws to their sovereign Ruler (I speak of those who are His subjects and vassals) to make men serve Him according to their tastes, and not according to His?

TIMOTHY: This would be making themselves lords, and not subjects, and masters instead of servants.

DANIEL: Would they themselves endure this from even the greatest of their subjects? However, there is not even such a comparison between God and them as there is between them and their subjects. For they are mortal men just as their subjects; they can sin as other men, and by the just judgment of God they can fall from their reign into servitude and subjection—indeed, often into the subjection and servitude of their own subjects—as has often happened to many because they did not wish to be subject to God, but instead sought to overthrow and rule above Him. These things cannot happen to God.

THE OFFICE OF GOOD RULERS AND GOOD SUBJECTS

TIMOTHY: Then it is not the office of a good ruler to seek to abolish the laws of religion given by God, or to prevent his subjects from following them, or to change them in order to give and establish others according to his own pleasure.

DANIEL: This is easy to see. But to the contrary, his office is to make his subjects observe them by all means possible for him. And, in order to give them a good example, he himself ought firstly to observe the laws given by God, and to regulate all of his laws by them. For he was ordained by God as a ruler for no other reason than this (Rom. 13:1-7; 1 Tim. 2:1-2). This is why the Lord commanded that the book of the Law be read before the king after he was elected, that he might know how to lead and govern according to its teaching, as well as the people who were given into his charge (Deut. 17:18-20).

TIMOTHY: If he must do this, he cannot ask his subjects to render him an honor that does not pertain to him at all, but he will instead desire that it be reserved for God, to whom alone it is due.

DANIEL: It is quite certain that if he knows well who he is, and if he understands his office well, he will not think that his subjects can show him any greater honor than honoring God as is required of them. For his honor is contingent upon God's. And he cannot fail to be well-honored and faithfully served by his subjects if God is well-honored and faithfully served both by him and them.

TIMOTHY: His subjects then would render him the greatest wrong and the greatest dishonor that can possibly be imagined if they gave him the honor which is not his due, and which he ought never to receive.

DANIEL: It is just as you say. For this would be placing him in the stead of God, and making an idol and a true devil of him, seeing that this is the honor which the devil always requires—that is, to be placed in the stead of God—as he has always shown from the beginning.

TIMOTHY: I can see this well.

HOW THOSE WHO OBEY THE LAWS WHICH FORBID MEN FROM SERVING GOD ARE OBEYING THE DEVIL AND NOT THEIR RULERS

DANIEL: Seeing that it is so, if we found a ruler with such presumption as formerly existed among the pagan emperors, kings, and rulers, and as the pope is today in Christendom by following their path and example, it is easy to see that his subjects would not be bound to obey him in this way any more than the devil himself, who is still a much greater ruler than all tyrants and all those who demand such honors. For he is called "the god of this world," "the prince of this world," and the ruler "of the darkness" (2 Cor. 4:4; John 12:31; Eph. 6:12). All these petty tyrants are no more than his subjects and vassals, and are as his little claws.

Therefore when the subjects are brought to such a necessity, they can justly use not only the same law as the apostles, who responded in such a case, "It is better to obey God than men," but could also say the same in other words, "It is better to obey God than the devil" (see Acts 4:19). For whoever obeys men against the commandment of God is obeying the devil, by whom they are possessed. For this reason they are also heirs of the same inheritance as the devil and his tyrants, whom they hold in greater fear than God.

LAWS AND STATUTES LAWFUL FOR CHRISTIAN RULERS, AND THE END TO WHICH THEY MUST LOOK IN THEM

TIMOTHY: I do not think that by what you say you wish to deny that it is lawful for rulers to give laws and ordinances to their subjects in conformity with the Word of God in order to induce them to true religion.

DANIEL: How could I condemn it when I said that this is their particular duty and office? For in doing this they themselves preach the Law of God. But what I said previously concerned laws and edicts which are made openly contrary to the Law of God, either to abolish it or to deform religion.

TIMOTHY: Those who do this are truly tyrants, and not rulers.

DANIEL: Do not doubt that Nebuchadnezzar, Darius, and Cyrus, these pagan emperors and kings who made such wondrous edicts to make public the knowledge of God throughout all their empires and kingdoms and who gave such assistance to the true servants of God, will rise up on the Day of Judgment and grievously condemn the rulers who claim the name of Christian and yet after so great a light of the Gospel have hindered the publication of the knowledge and will of God, for which these others labored (Dan. 3:28-29; 4:1-37; 6:25-27).

UNFAITHFUL SERVANTS WHO ARE IN RULER'S COURTS, AND THEIR COUNSELS AGAINST GOD; AND RULERS WHO PREFER SUCH SERVANTS OVER THOSE WHO HAVE RIGHTEOUS AND PURE HEARTS

TIMOTHY: It could be that there are Christian rulers who make edicts which they would never make if they had counselors within their courts similar to Daniel, Ezra, and Nehemiah, who led and incited them to glorify God's name, as these holy prophets and good servants of God did among those kings. But instead of having such, they often have quite the contrary, who prevent them (as much as they are able) from hearing and understanding the Word of God, and from learning by it what their true office is. These men do not cease to incite them to persecute the teaching which they themselves ought to maintain and advance.

DANIEL: This is no surprise, for such people often make use of rulers the same way huntsmen employ decoys. They handle religion as it pleases them, and however it appears will work better to further their ambition and fill their stomachs. And because they do not possess the power to give authority to their laws and to uphold their injustices, they abuse the power and authority of the rulers to do this, inducing them by their wicked and traitorous counsel to do whatever pleases them.

Now as these often take advantage of the ignorance and negligence of the rulers, so on the other hand the rulers often take advantage of the wicked spirits of such people, to make them serve their own ambition, tyranny, and evil schemes. Therefore they prefer them over more honest people, and could not endure them if they were otherwise and if they gave them faithful counsel, to the honor of God and the salvation of their souls and their subjects. They do this because they do not desire to obey God and to provide His people the liberty to serve Him, nor to reform the Church according to His Word, but rather they desire to pervert true religion in order that it might serve their ends, following the example of Jeroboam.

For this reason they much prefer prophets and priests similar to those of Jeroboam, Ahab, Jezebel, and Pharaoh's magicians, in order that they might have a better excuse for resisting the truth of God, that of the true servants of God, who follow in the footsteps of the true prophets and apostles. And because their people also desire such men and truly deserve to have such, God gives them what they request. But this is done in His wrath, as He threatened by His prophets, in order that they might have greater matter for hardening their hearts ever more and more, and to better hasten their ruin (Isa. 3:1-5; 29:9-12; Hosea 5:1-6; 7:13-14).

CHAPTER SEVEN

Jurisdictions and Callings Ordained by God

With the coming of the sixteenth century Reformation the call to return to Scripture as the absolute authority for all areas of life began to resonate throughout the countries touched by the Reformation. The authority claimed by the ecclesiastical heads of the Roman Catholic Church was questioned, weighed, and examined through the lens of Scripture. Much unbiblical teaching and many traditions were rejected as men sought to return to the truth of the Word, and Protestant churches found themselves restructuring the worship services and governmental structure of the church.

As reforms within the churches swept the Reformation towns, cities, and countries, certain men arose who attempted to restructure or revolutionize the civil government as well. Appealing to Scripture to justify their actions, they preached a gospel of insurrection and rebellion against the civil magistrates. Some men stated that no civil officers were legitimate unless they were Christians, while others declared that civil government itself was unnecessary and ought to be wholly abolished.

In the midst of the political turmoil and upheavals plaguing the peoples, many Protestant pastors strove to instruct their people in the Biblical doctrines of jurisdiction and submission to authorities. The following excerpt is one of Viret's writings intended to counter the revolutionary thinking of his day and to explain the jurisdictional bounds and differences between ministers of the Word, ministers of the sword (civil magistrates), and private individuals. Viret also addresses those who declare that they have a right to overthrow or usurp the authority of the civil magistrate because God has given them a special calling to do so.

At the end of the passage are a few paragraphs from the same work dealing with the necessity of employing a civil magistrate when waging war.

We must pay diligent heed to what our office and calling is, in order that we might not rashly undertake anything, and that we might not confuse the order that God has placed among men regarding the spiritual realm and the order that must exist in both His church and the temporal realm and civil order. We all have the commandment to hallow God's name, and we therefore daily pray that it might be hallowed. So on the other side we have been forbidden from dishonoring and soiling it, in whatever manner this might be done. But, though this is true, yet pastors and ministers of the church, according to their specific calling, have a particular charge different from that of the civil magistrates and others who are among the people (as well as the general calling which is common to all). They also have many means to serve to the glory of God, and various bounds and obligations much greater than what other people have. The same can be said of rulers, civil magistrates, all their officials, and other various positions and offices that exist among men for the maintaining of public order.

Therefore, following this line of thought, if it be a question of my person, I must firstly look to my general calling which I share in common with all believers. Then I must look to my particular calling, and seek to acquit myself of it as well as I am able. For inasmuch as I am a Christian, I am bound by all that a true Christian is bound by because of his profession of faith and his religion. But inasmuch as I am either a pastor or minister of the church, or a magistrate, public official, or have some other charge as a public man, or if I have no other office than that of a private individual, I am bound either more or less to do many things which others are not bound to as I am; or I am excused from doing certain things because of the position and calling that I have besides what is common and general to all (Rom. 12:3-6). For according to the gifts I have received from the Spirit of God and according to the means He has given me and the talents He has committed to me, I must be engaged in putting them to work, and I must also give an account of them (1 Cor. 12:4-7). And as much as I have received, so much greater an account will He require of me (Matt. 25:14-30).

If what I have said is well understood, it will be easy to see that whoever is a minister and pastor of the church must be the guide of the blind, lead the erring back to the way, and proclaim Jesus Christ to those who are under his charge (Matt. 28:18-20; Mark 16:15; Luke 24:27; Acts 1:8; 10:1-20). If he does not endeavor to do so, he must prepare himself for one of two things: either he must no longer meddle with being a pastor, and must no longer take his place among them, or he is preparing to give an account of the sheep under his charge to the Prince of pastors, who will require at his hands the blood of those who perish because of him (Eze. 3:17-21). Thus he owes more to the church than some simple man of the people who has not been given this charge or the gifts and means to do it.

It is enough for a common man to guard against soiling himself by idolatry or dishonoring God by wicked works, and to seek to honor Him by the means that God has given him according to his calling, in teaching his family well. But it is not enough for the man who is a pastor to only do this much, if he does not also labor for others, call them from straying, and instruct them in the knowledge of Jesus Christ, just as his office requires. But when he sets forth the doctrine and teaching which he ought, and when he himself is first to fulfill his duty in showing the way to others and in giving them a good example, for the rest he is neither bound nor obligated to take up the sword and arms and usurp to himself the office of the ruler, or to meddle in what is properly and particularly committed to the magistrate to maintain order among men. Thus it does not belong to him to go of his own authority and cast down and destroy idols and physically punish those who transgress the Word of God. For this is not the office of the ecclesiastical minister, and even less is it the office of a common man.

Thus it is enough for the minister to have fulfilled his office, and to have shown to men of all positions what they must do, and to have labored for the salvation of each one, as much as his office and the discipline of the church requires and allows. For the rest, he must leave to the magistrate what belongs to the magistrate. For the office of the magistrate is to abolish idols and all instruments of idolatry, and to remove the public offenses that are within the church, just as Hezekiah and Josiah did, according to the Word of God (2 Kings 18:1-6; 2 Chron. 29:1-11). His office is also to execute what is particularly given to his charge according to this Word. If the magistrate does not do this, the minister fulfills his duty when he condemns by the Word of God what it condemns, and when he points out and daily teaches both by word and deed to every man what he must do, and when he has fulfilled his charge as far as the discipline of the church extends.

The means of instructing for the edification of all lies in the wisdom that God gives to each one, of knowing how to prudently dispense the talents, mysteries, and secrets of the Kingdom of God which are committed to him. For just as Jesus Christ testified, the wise and prudent householder brings forth his provision in the proper time and place, and sets out new and old things. So also the wise ministers of the Gospel know how to set forth, administer, and distribute the teaching to their listeners according to their capacities and the edification of every man (Matt. 13:52). For He who gives ministers the knowledge and understanding of the Scriptures also gives them the grace to know how to make it understandable to the people whom God has given them. Seeing that the Spirit of God who speaks through us is the Spirit of wisdom, they cannot speak rightly if they are not led by this Spirit, and if they are not true servants of God and called by a lawful calling to the ministry of His Church (Matt. 10:20; Isa. 11:2-4). Thus let all ministers beware of quenching this Spirit and this gift of God, but let them arouse themselves by stirring up the gift of God which was given to them by prophecy, according to the admonition the apostle gave Timothy (1 Thess. 5:19; 1 Tim. 4:14).

Just as ministers are not bound to do what pertains to rulers and magistrates, so on the other hand if they do not sound the word, and do not speak to the rulers and magistrates with all frankness according to their calling, they will be guilty of grave guilt. For they would then be included in the number of dumb dogs which Isaiah speaks of. For their office requires them to call the rulers and magistrates to do their duty according to the Law of God. Therefore God commanded that when the king was elected and established in his reign, the book of the Law must be set before him and he must read it in order that he might learn to govern his people and his kingdom according to it (Deut. 17:18-20). To whom does it better pertain to set forth this book than to the true prophets of God?

Thus those who madly and recklessly, and without order and proper means, cast down idols, or put up some offensive placards, or do some other similar thing which in no way pertains to them and serves no other end than to stir up a great deal of trouble and a grievous persecution and to offend those who are not instructed in these matters, ought not to be praised, but are worthy of great censure, and particularly those who do this either out of thoughtlessness or vainglory, or out of rashness or inconsiderate zeal. And then, if they are taken in this, they deny and blaspheme Jesus Christ, as much as their adversaries desire, to save their life or to lessen or lighten their torments.

Daniel and his companions did not do this in Babylon. And likewise, in the times when idolatry reigned, the holy people who were among the children of Israel did not seek to destroy the idols of the idolaters by force in an attempt to stir up some insurrection. The prophets were content to preach against idolatry as their office required, or to show by proper means that this displeased them and that they did not approve of it. They left the office of destroying the idols and abolishing the offenses to those to whom the power of the sword was committed—that is, to the kings, rulers, and their officials to whom this pertains.

And if God did not give them magistrates who fulfilled their duty, nevertheless they persevered in their calling, which is to teach, rebuke, admonish, exhort, and correct by the Word of God. For the rest they waited for the Lord to provide what they could not correct on their own, either by means of some good ruler or in some other proper manner, such as was pleasing to God, to give them the occasion, without in any way confounding or perverting the order given by God. The other servants of God who were not prophets, and who did not hold a public office in the church, were in their place content to follow the teaching of the true prophets and to instruct their own families according to it. For even if we are not public ministers in the church, we nevertheless must each be so in our own houses and families toward our wives, children, servants, and handmaids, as were Abraham and all the other patriarchs (Gen. 17:9-10; 18:17-19).

Someone, in contradiction to what I have just said, might set forth firstly the example of Gideon, who cast down the altar and the idol to Baal in the night; and secondly the example of Rachel, who stole the gods from her father Laban; and thirdly the example of Phinehas, who killed the fornicator of the children of Israel, and his whore, and other such examples regarding these things (Judges 6:25-27; Gen. 31:19; Num. 25:1-14).

But it is easy to respond to these objections. For the first, we have a rule which teaches us that the examples and particular actions of the saints must not be taken as a conclusion of what we ought to do, or as a general rule. We must not easily depart from the general order simply for the sake of one or two examples.

Furthermore, what Gideon did, he did by the direct command of God and by a particular calling as a ruler or magistrate (Judges 6:25-26). For though he was not revealed as such before men (and particularly before those of his village who raised such a great complaint before his father against him), yet he was so before God. And therefore he was assured of his calling by Him, as Moses was assured of his when he killed the Egyptian (Ex. 2:11-12; Acts 7:23-25). For though at that time Moses was not publicly exercising the office of a magistrate, yet God who placed it in his heart to go to visit his brethren, also placed it in his heart to defend the innocent man against whom the Egyptian did wrong, and to mete out vengeance upon the Egyptian. In all his works he was led by the Spirit of God, such that this was for Moses as an entrance, to begin to take possession of the office for which God had prepared him. For God knew very well, and had revealed to Moses (though He had not revealed it to others) what He would afterward reveal in His time by His public testimony. And that he acted rightly Stephen assures us, who exposits this passage in the sense that I have said (Acts 7:23-25). Likewise the testimony that God gave him by the deliverance of His people, and by the other marvels that He did by the hand of Moses, confirms it to us.

Furthermore, in the village where Gideon was, it truly

appears by the complaint the inhabitants made to his father, that Gideon's father was held in great esteem, and that he was as a ruler or governor of the village. Otherwise they would instead have brought their complaint to the governors of their village. Therefore Gideon had some occasion and slight justification to do this more than others. Nevertheless he did not desire to do it without a certain calling from God, which God afterward publicly declared by the victory He gave him against the Midianites (Judges 7:15-23). And though he did all this, still he did this work at night, in order that there might be less tumult and uprising.

Concerning the example of Rachel, we do not read that Jacob consented to this or approved of it, but rather the opposite (Gen. 31:32). Regarding the example of Phinehas, we can say the same as Gideon. For God Himself declared that the act pleased Him (Num. 25:11-13). But if what he did were a general rule for all, it would follow that all the saints who did not do the same, and who still do not do so today, and who do not kill all those who blaspheme and offend God as those did, are worthy of great censure. And if it were so, there would be no order among men. The ecclesiastical minister would be confused and mixed with the civil magistrate, from which would follow a terrible confusion. Furthermore, every man would take the sword in hand according to his every whim. And then they would allege the example of Phinehas, Moses, Gideon, Elijah, and others like them (1 Kings 18:40). In short, whatever their leader told them would become for them the Spirit of God, as has happened with certain Anabaptists and Libertines. For there are some found among them who have gone as far as to kill each other—indeed, a brother has murdered his own brother. Others have stooped to fornication, without giving any heed to the Word of God, all just as their beastly desires lead them. They have done no more nor less than if all the wives were held in common, just as a herd of cows, mares, or sows are common to the bulls, horses, and boars that are mixed in with them. But God has, among other things, given us these good examples of this carnal and frenzied spirit begotten in the brain of the Libertines, and what fruits it bears in those who partake of it!

And therefore we must take heed and note what has already been said concerning the two types of callings which we have spoken of. There are two different types, which I call *special* and *particular*. (For the moment I leave off the general calling which is common to all inasmuch as it concerns the calling that is common to all children of God.) Concerning *particular* callings which deal with particular offices, there is one sort which is ordained by the common and general order God placed among men. This is the ordinary and most common. Therefore it is less easy to mistake, and less dangerous to be deceived.

There is another sort which we can call *extraordinary*, which is not as common as the other. This proceeds from a particular privilege of God, and a special revelation and calling which is not revealed to all (as is the ordinary, in which God uses His accustomed order), but it is only revealed to him who is called, until God reveals it to others by his authority, by evident signs, and by the assistance that He gives those whom He has called. We have examples of such callings in those of whom we have just spoken.

But there is a grave danger in this last sort of calling, that our flesh and our desires and emotions will deceive us and transport us in such a way that we believe them to be the Spirit of God. For there is a grave danger that Satan will transform himself into an angel of light, and that we will follow the devil instead of God, being deceived by a fanatic zeal without knowledge, or by our own desires or emotions. For we willingly make ourselves believe what we desire. And when Satan knows our fanatic desires, he pushes us as much as he can, in order that we might do some scandalous thing to hinder the course of the Word of God.

But if the calling is not of God, the fact will always be revealed in the end. We have examples of this in what happened previously, both in the time when Jesus Christ was manifested on earth and in the times of the apostles, in the Sadducees, Judas of Galilee, Theudas, the Egyptian, and others like them, of whom Josephus and the Acts of the Apostles make mention (Acts 5:17-18, 36-37; 21:37-38).

And even in our time we have the histories and examples of the peasants of Germany who were deceived by certain false prophets, and took up arms against their rulers and their feudal lords when the Gospel first began to be preached among them. We also have the Anabaptists of Munster and many other examples that would be too long to recount. The result has clearly revealed that the prophets of these people were false, and that their endeavors were not of God. For the sign that Moses gave to judge the prophets shows us this. He says that whenever a prophet prophesies or promises something, and what he prophesies does not come to pass, he is without doubt a false prophet, for he has lied (Deut. 18:20-22). For the Spirit of God cannot lie; but this proceeds from the devil, who is a liar and the father of lies (John 8:44).

These are examples that God has placed before our eyes in our own time in order that we might through others learn to rely on Him, to walk in His fear, and to beware of undertaking anything without His Word and a clear and certain calling. For if what Moses, Phinehas, Gideon, and the others did had a good end, it does not follow that we can do the same if God has not called us (as He did them) to the work that we undertake. And if He called them by an extraordinary calling and by a singular privilege (just as a sovereign ruler disposes of his servants and all matters pertaining to his kingdom as he judges to be the most expedient), it does not indeed follow that I am of this rank and order, and that God wills to employ me in such affairs simply because I desire it, or because I presume to take it upon myself. For rulers do not give offices and commissions to those who want them and who think themselves worthy of them, but to those who please them, or to those they know to be most suitable for the work in which they desire to employ them, and those who are the most fitting for it. And when God wills to call us to an extraordinary calling, He will reveal it to us so certainly that it will be impossible for us to have any doubts remaining.

Therefore let us beware of being too flippant, too presumptuous, and too overconfident and reckless. Let us heed the example of the servants of God, who were always in a great fear of undertaking anything—no matter how small the matter might be—without a clear calling from God. Therefore they did not dare to lay their hand to the task, even though God called them, without firstly being well assured, and without diligently enquiring whether the calling was from God or not, and without this calling being assured and confirmed either by signs and miracles or by some other seals which bore witness to the authority of God, both toward them whom He called as well as toward the others to whom they were sent. Seeing that it is so, what recklessness and arrogance would it be for us to run thoughtlessly forward and undertake matters of great importance without a certain calling and without assurance of the will of God? Let us beware of being reproached with the reproach the Lord gave the false prophets by Jeremiah: "I have not sent these prophets, yet they ran" (Jer. 23:21). We are assured that all that we undertake by a sure and certain calling of God, and according to His will, will have a good end. For when God sets us to a work, we must take it as assured that He will assist us. It is therefore impossible for the work not to prosper in our hands. For He is the true laborer, and the true workman, not us, who are no more than His tools. But the tool which is in the hand of such a workman cannot fail to accomplish a good work. For nothing can hinder Him.

But if we undertake something without Him and

without His Spirit, it is quite certain that He will reproach us as He reproached the Jews by His prophet Isaiah: "[They] take counsel, but not of Me; and that cover with a covering, but not of My Spirit" (Isa. 30:1). It is certain that in such a case we will accomplish nothing worth doing, and will undertake nothing except what will lead to our confusion and ruin.

NECESSITY OF A MAGISTRATE WHEN WAGING WAR

But it is even more wicked for us to trust in our own arms and power, and to take up arms against our persecutors if we are not called of God by a lawful and certain calling. And if this is wicked, it is even worse if we boast of our arms and strength when God has given us some little victory against them, and when He has transformed our folly and rashness into something that brings Him honor and glory.

For, firstly, if we are not magistrates, and if we do not have magistrates or captains who have been ordained by God to defend us against the abuses of the persecutors, we must not take up any other arms to withstand the attacks of this battle than those with which Jesus Christ has armed us. He said, "I send you forth as sheep in the midst of wolves: be ye therefore wise as serpents, and harmless as doves. But beware of men.... But when they persecute you in this city, flee ye into another." And, "In your patience possess ye your souls" (Matt. 10:16-17, 21; Luke 21:19).

He did not say, "I send you forth as wolves against wolves," or as bears against lions. If we wish to have Jesus Christ for our Shepherd, we are required to be sheep, not wolves. For He is not a Shepherd of wolves, but of sheep. If we are sheep, we must endure afflictions, not cause them. And therefore Jesus Christ arms us with patience. Now there is no need for patience until there is also affliction and offense.

CHAPTER EIGHT

Using the Magistrate for Good

If we are in a place in which we might be aided by the laws, customs, liberties, and franchises either of the country or of the magistrates in a way that would make them serve to God's cause—which we strive toward—or if we can have some other good means besides, we can use them as Paul used these means:

When Paul was in Ephesus at the time of the great riot and the great insurrection which was started by Demetrius and the other silversmiths, he indeed wanted to go throw himself into the midst of the tumult in order to quiet it. But he did not despise the counsel of the brethren, who prevented him from going there and who kept him confined and hidden in their houses until the insurrection was appeased (Acts 19:24-41). For there was at the time neither order nor means for the Gospel to profit in such a fury of the people.

And when he was a prisoner of Lysias in Jerusalem, he was warned by his nephew of the plot that certain of the Jews had made against him, and how they had sworn to kill him, and had taken a vow that they would neither eat nor drink until they had taken his life. He did not despise this warning, though his nephew who had heard them was no more than a young child. Neither did he send to the believers and ask them to execute some evil plot against these murderers. But he sent his nephew to Lysias to inform him of this scheme and the treachery they thought to use to put him to death, in order that he might appeal to him as a just magistrate who was ordained for the defense of the innocent (Acts 23:16-22).

When Lysias understood this intrigue, and when he knew that the Jews had determined to send and request that Paul be sent to them to appear before their counsel, in order that they might treacherously murder him by the way under the guise of wishing to hear him, he put his soldiers in good order, well mounted and well armed. Then he gave Paul into their charge, ordering them to safely carry and conduct him by night to Caesarea, and to hand him over to the provost Felix and deliver him by this means from this danger (Acts 23:23-24). Paul did not refuse this means, nor did he refuse to be taken by night under arms by pagan soldiers and men-at-arms from the garrison at Jerusalem, sent by order of the captain of the city, to avoid the ambushes of his enemies. But he did nothing against God by appealing to this aid. He did not obtain it by evil means. Nor did he wish to remain and tempt God, without requesting the captain's aid against this treachery. For the warning that he made aspired to no other thing. And God did not warn him of this danger by his nephew for any other reason. He did his duty, and then he left the charge of the means to God, who inspired the captain to do as he did; and Paul had no reason to be sorry.

Likewise, when he was before Felix and Festus the Roman governors, and before King Agrippa, he lawfully remained and defended his cause against his enemies, as a true advocate and lawyer. He was served by the art of rhetoric, by all civility and honesty, and by the laws and customs which could lawfully serve him in his cause.

When he was brought before the Jewish council, and when he realized that there was no hope of finding any justice or equity among them, but that he stood in the midst of them as a sheep among wolves, knowing that they were grouped in sects and opinions (as our doctors of the Sorbonne and our monks are today), and that they bore such a love for each other as do dogs and cats (and as our monks do today), he made use of their discord. He placed them in dissension against each other in order that he might escape from their hands and might find some favor by telling the truth, without however causing any harm or injury to any of them or to the church. For he spoke nothing but the pure truth. The discord came from among themselves, and not from him. If they had already been in agreement among themselves, and truly united in the doctrine of God and in a true faith and love, and had he then caused a dissension among them, he would have sinned greatly. But he did not cause any new disagreements. He did not thrust in his lance to divide them in doctrine and to break their unity in the truth of God. For this had already been done. But because he saw them all united against him to do him evil and to destroy the teaching of Jesus, he only sought to break this evil union that they had to do evil. And taking the occasion to do this from the diversity of their opinions, he sought to win the Pharisees if he could (who followed the most sound opinion), and to make them reject that of the Sadducees (which was false), and thus escape from their hands. He displayed great wisdom in being able to protect the truth of God entire, without lying, and to find such a means of escape. For because he preached Jesus Christ resurrected and the resurrection in His name, he could with just reason say that he was called into judgment because of the resurrection, seeing that he was called for the teaching of Jesus Christ. And by this means he gave occasion to the Pharisees to look more kindly upon his cause, and to draw nearer to Jesus Christ, seeing that His teaching was not as contrary to theirs as was that of the Sadducees.

On the other hand, he did not openly declare that he was there because of Jesus. For they would not have had the patience to hear him, and the cause would not have been as favorable. Yet he did not deny this; he simply did not say it openly.

And when Festus wished to send him back to the Jews, Paul, knowing their wickedness, and that he would find less justice among them than before the cruelest tyrants of the earth, appealed to the emperor, and was carried to Rome (Acts 25:10-11).

Thus we see how Paul made use of the magistrates and their officials—indeed, even of pagans and unbelievers—and of their civil laws and human assistance and occasions, as good creatures of God, when God gave him the means to do so.

Thus if you are in a country in which someone does you an injury, you can have recourse to the magistrate of the place if the matter is worthy of it, and if it requires it, and if you can do this by honest means, without dishonoring God and without violating the love you owe to your neighbor.

If you do this, not out of a desire for revenge, but with such an intention (as we have shown above) as Paul had, and which we must also have, you do not sin. If the evildoer receives some damage, you did not seek this; this is not the end to which you aimed by having recourse to the magistrate. This is not by you, but by the magistrate; not by your fault, but by his. For you do not desire evil upon your enemy, but his amendment and his good. Thus it is not you who has worked vengeance, but God. For when you deliver vengeance to the magistrate, you return it to God who ordained him to this work and this end. And what you do is not done out of a desire for revenge, but only to deliver yourself from the tyranny of the evildoer.

And if you could do this by some other means which would be more profitable, you would willingly do so. But when it must be that either you suffer from him unjustly, or that he suffers justly from the magistrate, you are not bound to abandon your just cause for his wicked one, and to give more favor to his wicked cause than to your just one, seeing that you only employ the means that God has given you—indeed, even as by constraint and by the importunity of your enemy, who has forced you to employ such a remedy.

Now if this is permitted to Christians, there is no doubt that the poor believers who are tormented and tyrannized among the Roman Catholics also have good reason to praise God if they have some friends around their kings and rulers who desire to favor and assist them in their court, or if they have some officials who bear them favor. For they must acknowledge the favor that God shows them by this means. They can use it as Daniel, Ezra, Nehemiah, Mordecai, Esther, and Paul used it, but only as long as they observe the conditions which these observed, as has already been written above. And if the unbelieving rulers, magistrates, and pagan officials bore some favor to these good servants of God, it will be a great shame to those who are in the courts, and who have the means to assist their brethren (and particularly those who know the truth), if they do not at least do as much for them as these pagans did in their ignorance for those who held a religion contrary to their own.

Likewise we can sometimes use concealed speech when we see that it will in no way be profitable to speak the truth openly. But we must beware of lying. We can also make the divisions of the enemies of the truth serve by occasion to break their power and their schemes against the Gospel when we can do so by honest means, without calumny, without lying, and without committing any act unworthy of a Christian, just as Paul did. We can also justly refuse, and flee the courts and judgments of wicked judges and those from whom we can expect the least justice and favor because of the cause of Truth, and seek out others and call upon other places, if we have the means to do so according to God. For though Paul was a Jew, yet, knowing the perversity of his nation and of the priests and doctors of Jerusalem, he preferred to appear before pagans instead of them, though he did not look to this only, but also to the fact that he desired an opportunity of going to Rome, as had already been revealed to him by God (Acts 25:10-11).

CHAPTER NINE

When Can Christians Wage War?

Now, because we have already condemned those who without a particular calling of God take up arms either against their rulers or against others, someone might ask whether it is ever lawful to take up arms against persecutors for the defense of the Gospel. There are many things to consider on this question.

We must first consider the state in which we find ourselves and the means that God has given us. For it is not lawful for anyone except magistrates to take up arms. For God did not give the sword to bear to any other besides him (Rom. 13:4). He has forbidden all vengeance to men, and has reserved it for Himself, saying, "Vengeance is Mine; I will repay" (Deut. 32:41; Rom. 12:19). Thus, seeing that He has reserved vengeance for Himself, we ought truly to beware of seeking to usurp what He has reserved for Himself, and what pertains to Him alone. He will not allow us to despoil Him of His jurisdiction or of His right and office. For if an earthly ruler will not allow someone to come up and ascribe to themselves the office that belongs to him alone, or if he will not permit another man to do the office that he has committed to his officials other than his officials themselves, we must not think that God the sovereign Lord of all will any more permit such an offense to be done Him.

Thus, seeing that He has reserved to Himself this right of lordship and that He is our sovereign Lord, it is not lawful for any man to put his hand to this work except Him and His officers alone—that is, those to whom He has given this charge. The men to whom He has given this charge are the magistrates, whom He has armed with the sword, and has entrusted it to them (just as a ruler entrusts it to his officers) when He called them to this office, as Isaiah testifies in speaking of Cyrus the king of Persia. The Lord stated clearly by His prophet that He armed Cyrus, and that He buckled his belt, girded his loins, and put a sword upon his thigh in order to work vengeance against the tyrants who abused His people, and to deliver His servants (Isa. 45:1-5). For, since God has forbidden murder and any harm done against our neighbor in any form whatever, whoever does the contrary offends God. But when the magistrate acts in God's name and defends the good and punishes the wicked, he is not acting in his own name or by his own authority, but by the authority and commandment of God (Gen. 9:6; Ex. 20:13; Matt. 5:21). And therefore it is not he who acts, but God who acts through him, for the magistrate is no more than His minister and servant (Rom. 13:4).

If a criminal kills a man for his own pleasure, he will be taken as a criminal and punished as a criminal. Furthermore, if a man kills another, even though the man he killed was also a wicked man and worthy of death, nevertheless he who killed him on his own authority without possessing either charge or commission from his ruler, even though he killed the other man because of the crimes he had committed, yet he will still be taken for a murderer and punished as a murderer (if the ruler does not show him clemency). For he did not possess this charge or this authority.

If every man were permitted to kill those who deserved it, we would have a slaughterhouse instead of an earth. There would be a horrible confusion. For every man would judge his neighbor worthy of death according to his own whim. Each would work his particular revenge under this cover. And for this reason God willed that there be a good order in such things. He willed that the wicked be punished, but He did not choose for this to be done by those to whom the injury was made in particular, and who were most closely affected by the wrong. For there would always be a danger that these people might proceed beyond measure, and would labor to serve their own desires and revenge, instead of the will of God and the restoration and salvation of the evildoer. And therefore God willed that those who would judge in such a case would be neutral, in order that they might not be inclined to one side or the other, but that they might have a just judgment. Yet He was not even content with this. But, because it is very difficult for a man to take such measures as is required in such a case, and seeing that it is difficult not to overstep the bounds of justice or to be mistaken, and that he not do someone harm, being deceived either by avarice or by ignorance and all sorts of corruptions which exist among men, God willed that all judgment and all vengeance be regulated according to the just and equitable laws He gave to all people who fear Him. Thus, seeing that the magistrate is as the soul of the Law and the one who must give life and properly value the Law's authority, he will not be reproved, either by God or man, when he carries out his office according to the laws to which he himself is subject. For he does nothing but what is commanded him by his sovereign Ruler, as the officer of justice who executes the sentence of the judge. But if a private individual attempts to do the same without having this charge, he will be reproved, unlike the magistrate, who is praised. For we must never undertake anything without a lawful calling.

Thus if it happened that some tyrant rose up against the Gospel, if I am one of his subjects and he has dominion over me, I must be very careful lest I rebel against him presumptuously or rashly. I must pay close attention to how I am his subject. For there are some who are wholly subject, and others who, though subject, yet enjoy certain liberties, some more and some less, which their supreme rulers have promised and vowed to uphold. These have their own magistrates to protect them in their liberties and freedoms. Thus, just as there is a difference between various states and domains, so also there is a difference in the manner of taking up arms. Those who are wholly subject, so much so that they have among them neither magistrate nor ruler to lead them except the tyrants who persecute them, nor lawful means to resist them without placing the church and the country in much greater danger than if they patiently endured the persecutions, such people must recognize that God wills to prove them by the cross, and that He has given them these tyrants either to humble and chastise them for their sins, or to display the patience and steadfastness of His servants. Therefore they must follow the example of the people of God when they were in captivity without lawful magistrates, and take up the arms that they employed, to be delivered from the tyranny of the tyrants, as we declared in another place.[1]

But if it is a people who have their own laws, liberties, and magistrates, and who render their duty to those who can claim some lordship over them, and despite this, some tyrant comes who instead of abiding by what he has promised and vowed, and instead of doing his duty as his office requires, he seeks to tyrannize those whom he ought to favor, this is another matter. Therefore if such a people possess a lawful means to resist the tyranny of such tyrants by their legitimate magistrates, and are able by this means to avoid slavery, they can follow the counsel of Paul (which we previously spoke of) who said, "Let every man abide in the same calling wherein he was called. Art thou called being a servant? care not for it: . . . For he that is called in the Lord, being a servant, is the Lord's freeman" (1 Cor. 7:20-22). He adds, "but if thou mayest be made free, use it rather" (1 Cor. 7:21).

---
[1] See chapter eleven of this volume

We have many examples of what I say in many countries where the people enjoy great liberties and freedoms. For they are like their own lords, except for some little acknowledgement they owe to certain rulers. But when they have fulfilled this, they owe them nothing further. But they have their own natural-born rulers who have charge of their communities, and their own magistrates and officials who moreover have the whole charge of them. Thus if it happens that a ruler (to whom by right they are not subject) transformed himself into a tyrant, and was not content with what was his due and what was rendered to him, but sought by tyranny, force, and violence to destroy the Gospel, religion, and the liberty of the country, and like a Turk to destroy those whom he ought to protect as his children, then the people must seek to defend themselves against his tyranny by the best means God has given them. There is no doubt that in such a case the rulers and magistrates who exist are bound to defend themselves, their people, and the country which God has placed under their charge against such tyranny and violence.

And when the rulers do not do this, they are traitors and disloyal to God, their country, and to the people whom He has committed to them. For they are more bound to God (who raised them to their present state) and to the people who receive them in good faith, and who render them the obedience due them under God, than to the tyrants and criminals who were not received in good faith either by God or men, but come as wild beasts to destroy God's inheritance and to devour His sheep. Thus good rulers and magistrates are required to show themselves shepherds in such a case.

We could say the same of those who are subjects of the Turks. There are two types of these. The first are those who have been taken by force and who are wholly subject to them, as poor slaves. Thus they have no means of taking up arms against them. Therefore they can do nothing but endure the tyranny with all patience, and die rather than deny Jesus Christ and consent to the abominations of Mohammed, awaiting their deliverance just as the people who were in Egypt and Babylon.

There are others who, since they could not resist the power of the Turks, surrendered to them upon the condition that they might be permitted to live in the Christian religion and according to their own laws and manner of life, according to which they agreed with their enemies by a treaty of peace to pay them tribute and render homage to the Turks as it was imposed upon them. As long as the Turks keep the terms they promised, these people are also bound to keep what they promised, as Jeremiah declared to Zedekiah and those at Jerusalem who, after the city was taken the first time by the Babylonians, were left in the country under such conditions as I have just said.

But if the Turks break their word, and seek by tyranny to oppress the Christians who are subject to them and to constrain them to renounce Jesus and live according to the law of Mohammed, such subjects owe no further allegiance to such rulers, but can make use of the means God has given them, and can with their magistrates take up arms against such tyrants and oath-breakers.

For if it is lawful to administer justice to the innocent and to punish the wicked, and if magistrates are ordained for such a reason, it is also lawful to wage war for a just cause. For if the war is fought for a just cause, justice is on the side of the righteous. For if it is lawful to defend an innocent man from the violence of a wicked man, it is even more lawful to defend a thousand innocents and to punish a thousand wicked (and as many more as come), if God gives the means to do so. Thus there is scarcely any difference between a war and the ordinary justice which is rendered to evildoers except for the fact that, because in war there is a much greater horde of those who wish to do violence, so it is also required to have a much greater mass of servants for a magistrate, to serve him as his officers in resisting the power and violence of the enemies. Therefore the order of ordinary justice cannot be kept exactly.

Now if it is lawful to take up arms in such a case, it is even more lawful to take them up against those who are less bound to us, and who have less justifications or reasons, and who seek to abolish and wholly destroy Christianity.

But it is truly necessary to carefully examine these things with all diligence and in great fear of God. We are required to do all we can to preserve peace and to guard against ever taking up arms unless necessity constrains us in such a way that it is no longer possible to have peace, or unless peace would be worse and more damaging to the church and the country than war and death itself. If there is more profit to peace than to war, we must leave war to the wild animals.

And if we must have war, those who uphold the righteous cause must walk in all fear of God. We must maintain such discipline as the good kings God gave to His people kept in the wars they waged to defend the cause of God against the enemies of His people. This point ought to be treated more fully, but I have no room for it at present. For the moment it will suffice to have touched upon it in passing, in order that we might judge other similar cases.

What induced me to make some mention of this matter is because I have often heard that some of those who live under tyrants are always quick to take up arms against their enemies if anyone will counsel them to do so. Thus I truly desired to give the warning which I believe to be in accordance with God's Word regarding this point. And because I have condemned those who rashly take up arms without a particular calling, in order that it might not appear that I sought to generally condemn all those who have just cause to take up arms, and who have at times taken them up against the tyrants and persecutors of the church, I indeed wished to add this remonstrance to the preceding, and show the difference which can exist in such matters according to the times, places, persons, occasions, and offices of each man.

But above all, the main thing that I desire to be well considered on this matter is that all war is very dangerous and full of uncertainty, and that there is nothing which Christians ought to hold in greater horror than the taking up of arms—not only against Christians, but against all men upon the earth; and that there is nothing in which Christians ought to be more hesitant to engage, nor which agrees less with their profession of faith.

I also desire on these things that Christians always bear in mind that the church of Jesus Christ and His Kingdom is not a civil or earthly kingdom, but a spiritual; and that Jesus Christ has not given His church physical arms either to advance and increase it or to preserve and defend it, but instead it has always enjoyed a greater triumph over its enemies by means of the cross and persecutions than in prosperity (2 Cor. 10:3-4). This has been the means by which God has always preserved this spiritual Kingdom and caused it to triumph in this world over all His enemies. For from the beginning of the world all those who have waged war against it have met their end, and have all perished miserably. To the contrary, the Kingdom of Jesus Christ and His Church have always remained in the end, and shall remain forever and ever.

And still in our times we daily see that those who seek to increase and maintain this Kingdom by arms of flesh scarcely profit it at all, and that its power is better shown where there is less human strength. For it is truly difficult to have force and human aid without confiding in them more than we ought. And where this confidence of carnal arms exists, we must not expect any great feats or any other fruit than what Jeremiah the prophet promised us, saying, "Cursed be the man that trusteth in man, and maketh flesh his arm, and whose heart departeth from the Lord. For he shall be like the heath in the desert, and shall not see when good cometh; but shall inhabit the parched places in the wilderness, in a salt land and not inhabited." But to the contrary, "Blessed is the man that trusteth in the LORD, and whose hope the LORD is. For he shall be as a tree planted by the waters, and that spreadeth out her roots by the river, and shall not see when heat cometh, but her leaf shall be green; and shall not be careful in the year of drought, neither shall cease from yielding fruit (Jer. 17:5-8; Ps. 1:1-4; 91:9-12).

As a testimony to this we have all the examples of Holy Scripture. For by what hand and by what power were Pharaoh, all the people of the land of Canaan, and all the enemies of Joshua, David, Hezekiah, and the people of God overthrown? Who cast out the Edomites, Moabites, Ammonites, Philistines, Midianites, Amalekites, Syrians, Assyrians, Chaldeans, Persians, Medes, Greeks, Romans, Goliath, Sennacherib, and all the others tyrants of the earth with all their monarchies, empires, kingdoms, and domains? And who delivered the church from their tyranny? Was it the power of a physical sword?

What appearance was there that by this means the sheep might vanquish the wolves, foxes, dogs, swine, bulls, unicorns, tigers, leopards, bears, and lions? Thus we must look to none but to Him who said, "Behold, I send you forth as sheep in the midst of wolves" (Matt. 10:16). Indeed, in this lies all our consolation. If He had only said, "Go forth as sheep in the midst of wolves," we would have had great reason to be dreadfully afraid, and to turn back. But when He says, "Behold, it is I who send you forth," He assures us that, since it is He who sent us, He as the Shepherd has the care of those He sends, and He will guard them in such a way that no one will snatch them out of His hand (John 10:27-29). Therefore always bear this word in mind: "Behold, I send you." And, having such a Shepherd, let us leave the wolves to their raging, and fear them not, though we be surrounded by them.

Let us consider and always remember that great armies have never cast down the church of the Lord, but to the contrary they have always been destroyed by a small hand, and with a small number. Consider what comparison there was between the weapons of Egypt and those of the Israelites, and what equality there was between the armies and force of the Canaanites and those of Joshua (Ex. 14:5-16; 15:1-6; Josh. 8:1-2). Compare also the Midianites with Gideon, and Sisera with Barak, and Saul, Absalom, and Goliath with David, and Sennacherib with Hezekiah, and Antiochus with the Maccabees, and the forces and armies of each of them with the others (1 Sam. 17:1-24; 18:20-27; 2 Kings 19:32-37). Now consider what similarity there was in such things among the poor church of the Lord and all the rest of the world, and in all times.

Remember and consider the war of the Israelites against the Benjamites because of the Levite's concubine (Judges 20:1). The Israelites had a just cause, and undertook the war to fulfill their duty according to the counsel and will of God. They were without comparison a much greater number than their enemies. There were ten tribes against one; a thousand to one. The camp followers of their army were more numerous than Benjamin's entire army. Their enemies were no more than a handful of men. One tribe against ten, defending such a wicked and villainous cause. And yet those who had the best cause and who followed the counsel of God, and who were the most numerous and the strongest, were twice defeated and vanquished by their enemies. In those two times they lost forty thousand men: twenty-two thousand one time, and eighteen thousand the next.

And though all Israel was assembled together against them without any dissension or rebellion as though they were all one man, yet they never obtained the victory against their enemies until they humbled themselves before God by fastings and prayers, and asked pardon for their sins, and placed their pride and their glory under their feet (Judges 20:26). And then, when they had wholly rejected their own power and might, and had placed all their trust in God instead of in their great multitude and in their horses and weapons, and gave Him all the glory, they learned by experience that He is not without good reason called the Lord of Hosts. For though they had a righteous cause, and though God was with them and they had every advantage, even according to worldly standards, nevertheless God desired to humble them. For He resists the proud, but gives grace to the humble (1 Pet. 5:5; James 4:6). Now the Israelites were so prideful before they humbled themselves that it seemed to them that they could swallow their enemies whole and do what they wanted with them.

Therefore God willed to show them that victory lies neither in force of arms, nor in the multitude of men, nor even in a righteous cause, but in Him alone. For we can indeed take a cause which is righteous before God and make it a wicked one by our guilt and sins, and by what we add of ourselves. We have here a very clear example of this, and also in the victory of those of Ai against the people who were under Joshua (Josh. 7:1-5). For though the people of God had a just cause, yet they were smitten by their enemies and turned to flight only because of the sacrilege committed by Achan, which none of the other people were guilty of.

Now if God thus willed to punish this sacrilege in His people (who were not even guilty of it), and would not give them the victory until this sacrilege were removed from the midst of them, we ought not to be amazed if God often gives the victory to our enemies, seeing that so many abominations reign among us, of which we are all guilty; and that there are so many people whose hands are all stained and polluted with sacrileges, with plundering of the poor, and are guilty of the blood of the innocents. Are we astonished if for a time God gives us as prey to our enemies, no matter how righteous a cause we might have? For though we are no more than a handful of people and have all the world against us, yet we can still be united together; but we are so divided and so polluted by the affairs of this world that it is difficult to find even two who agree well with each other.

Now while such things were done, and while the people of God were treated in such a manner, what did the citizens of Ai and the Benjamites do? Doubtless they thought that they had obtained a full victory, and lit great bonfires and boasted of their wickedness—particularly the Benjamites and the Gibeonites. But this joy did not last long. To the contrary, it was the harbinger of their approaching doom; which was such in those of Ai, that not one of them remained—or at least the number was very small of those who survived their defeat (Josh. 8:24-25). And of the Benjamites, the tribe was almost wholly annihilated.

Thus we must not be surprised at the prosperity of the wicked or the violence of the Antichrist, but we must always bear in mind what Daniel said of him and all his henchmen: "he shall be broken without hand" (Dan. 8:25). Therefore when the times seem most desperate according to men, and when power and human might can least resist, God will bring down His power, which will be a vengeance so appalling that all the earth will stand amazed. Thus we have need of nothing more than to continually keep our eyes of faith raised to our Captain, who said, "Be of good cheer; I have overcome the world" (John 16:33).

CHAPTER TEN

True Obedience to Magistrates: Examples from Scripture

Now, because we have already previously mentioned the submission and obedience which believers owe to rulers, magistrates, and to all those whom God has given them as authorities and governors, and likewise the assistance and favor that the true servants of God ought to give each other by all possible means, I will now set before you some examples to illustrate this matter.

When the people of Israel were held captive in Egypt under the tyranny of Pharaoh, Moses records that, among the other cruel edicts which Pharaoh made against this people, he expressly commanded the midwives who received the children of the Hebrew women to kill all the male children at childbirth. But the midwives did not obey this cruel command. Therefore shouldn't they rightly be condemned for rebellion and disobedience against their king and ruler? But to the contrary Moses does them the honor of saying that they did not execute the command given them by the king because they feared God (Ex. 1:17). By this he clearly shows that they obeyed the true King and Ruler—not only of Egypt, but also of the entire earth—by disobeying Pharaoh, that cruelest of tyrants. And by the same means he teaches us that instead of the true servants of God being required to obey the edicts and commands which tyrants make against the Word of God, to the contrary, they receive great praise from the Spirit of God when they do not obey them at all. Also, they cannot rightly be regarded as true servants of God if they do obey them. For they cannot be true servants of God unless they fear God more than men.

If they fear God more than men, they will have a greater fear of disobeying and offending Him than of disobeying and offending men, no matter how great the kings and rulers might be. For there are none so grand nor so powerful and fearsome as He. And because the Israelite midwives feared Him more than they feared Pharaoh, the Lord gave them the recompense and reward He has promised to all who fear Him. For Moses particularly says that God blessed them because of this (Ex. 1:21). It is likewise true that, if they had served the tyranny of Pharaoh as he desired, he would have recompensed them as tyrants reward the ministers of their tyranny and their servants who obey them in it. But it was not in the power of Pharaoh to reward them and grant them such blessings as the Lord gave them. For he could not give them wages which would not afterward be counted truly costly if they had consented to such a cruel tyranny, and to be murderers of newborns in order to avoid the wrath of Pharaoh and gain his good favor.

True it is that there was a weakness in them in that they did not openly resist such cruelty, and did not frankly declare that they would not fulfill the office of executioners against the commandment of God. But to the contrary they employed lies (or at least deception) to excuse themselves before the king. But, though there was such a fault in their action (which was worthy of great censure before God), nevertheless God pardoned them, and did not fail to recognize the good they showed His poor people in the time of their greatest affliction.

Thus we must here consider the great goodness and lovingkindness of God toward us, in that He bears with us in our infirmities and our imperfections, and does not fail to find pleasure in the services we render to His children and servants out of the fear, love, and reverence we bear Him. Therefore we ought not to doubt, if He will support us in this point, that as much as He takes pleasure in such works, so much more ought we to labor more freely and frankly in them.

We likewise read that Pharaoh imposed taxes and burdens upon the children of Israel which it was not possible for them to fulfill. And yet he ordered his taskmasters who had the charge of overseeing the Israelites, commanding that they complete the tasks which were assigned them by the king each day (Ex. 5:6-9). The Egyptian taskmasters then ordered the others under them, who were taken from among the Israelites themselves. But, because these poor people were overburdened, the officers who were under the Egyptians did not render a full account to the Egyptians of the tasks which were required of the Israelites each day. And therefore the Egyptians took the Israelite officers and struck and beat them because they did not force and press their brethren the Israelites enough to fulfill the task which was assigned to them. These officers, finding themselves so treated, were constrained to appeal to Pharaoh and make their remonstrances for the wrong done to them and their brethren because what was demanded of them was impossible, seeing that they were charged with more than they could bear. Therefore they made their request to Pharaoh, asking him to take into consideration the fact that these poor people were overburdened.

Though no good came from the remonstrance and request these Israelite officers made to Pharaoh, and though they were as ungrateful to Moses and Aaron as were the other Israelites (as appears from the complaints they themselves made against them), yet they are to be praised because they preferred to receive blows themselves and to be beaten rather than press their poor brethren beyond measure. They obeyed Pharaoh and the Egyptians in all that they could obey them without violating their duty and their office. For though Pharaoh and the Egyptians did harm to the people of Israel by compelling them to labors and tasks that were neither just nor equitable, however, seeing that it was only a matter of physical things in which the Israelites could obey the king without damaging their conscience, the officers could also obey him in the charge which was given them as long as the poor people were able to fulfill it. For, because they were subjects of the king just as the others, they were also bound to obey and serve him as much as they could without clearly violating the Word of God. But they were not obligated to serve Pharaoh and the Egyptians when they demanded of the poor people more than what they could do. For this was tyranny upon tyranny, which the officers could not be ministers of without doing damage and violence to their brethren, against their duty and office of love.

This example can serve us against two types of people. For the first, there are some who are of so perverse a nature that, instead of relieving those who are afflicted by the tyrants they serve, they are not content to press the poor afflicted ones as far as the tyrant commands them, but go still further, as if they took great pleasure in the tyranny of their masters and lords. Some do this because they are inhuman and cruel by nature, and are enemies of God and all virtue. Others do it to please the tyrants, in order that they might be further advanced in their court and in their service.

There are others who are not led by such desires, but to the contrary have some pity and compassion on the poor children of God whom they see afflicted. There are even those who are not only moved with compassion toward them, but also willingly relieve them, if they can do so without putting themselves in any danger or without costing themselves anything. But this is not enough. For if we only aid the servants of God when we can do so without any peril or damage to our earthly goods or our own persons, we have no greater love for them than the pagans themselves require in all human and carnal friendship. For true Christian love (which God requires of us by His Law) requires us to be lacking in nothing of what is our duty and office, and that we do nothing against it, whatever might happen either to our own body or our earthly goods. For as Jesus Christ laid down His life for us out of obedience to God His Father, and to display the great love He bears us, so also we must give our lives for each other and follow His example when necessity requires it, just as John teaches us (John 13:34-35; 1 John 3:16).

We can add to the preceding examples that of Rahab, who is greatly renowned in the Holy Scriptures for the aid she rendered to the Israelite spies who were sent to Jericho by Joshua (Josh. 2:1). Because she was of the city of Jericho and from the country of the Canaanites, to whom was she more bound and obliged, both according to the laws of nature as well as the laws and statutes of all lords and countries, than to her own country and her natural lords? Yet she received and lodged in her own house the spies who had come to spy out the city and the country, and to drive out the inhabitants and totally destroy them.

Whoever sought to judge Rahab's deed according to human reason and judgment, and according to the laws and customs of every country and lordship, could say nothing except that she was disloyal to her own nation, and that she had betrayed her own country. For she was not unaware that they were spies. Nor was she ignorant of the reason why they had come there. For the news was so well known by the whole city that they searched for these spies in every place in order to apprehend them. Indeed, they even searched in Rahab's own house. But she said that they were not there. And yet they were there; but she had hidden them in a secret place until she found an opportunity and means to smuggle them out of the city without danger (as she afterward did, lowering them with cords through a window in her house, by which they could get outside the city walls). If what she did had been discovered by the king and the other lords and citizens of the city, she would doubtless have been condemned as an enemy of the city and the entire country, and she would probably have paid with her life.

Nevertheless, as much as it appears that she should have been condemned by the Word of God for doing this, to the contrary she is greatly praised, and afterward received a very great reward. For firstly, the Spirit of God bears witness that what she did here was done in faith (Heb. 11:31; James 2:25). For she did not save and deliver the spies she had lodged in her house from danger as a harlot would who desired to save her fornicators. For they did not go there to lodge with her to commit fornication as in a brothel. She likewise did not lodge them as a harlot to commit harlotry with them; though previously she had been taken for such, and had led an evil life. For she is called a harlot in the Holy Scriptures (Josh. 2:1; Heb. 11:31; James 2:25).

All this came to pass by the providence of God, who sent the spies to her. And the fact that she received and saved them proceeded from the fear of God within her, and from the faith she had in the promises God had made to the children of Israel, as clearly appears both by the conversation she had with the spies, as well as by the covenant she made with them, not only for her person, but also for all her house and all her family. Thus what human reason and earthly men call disloyalty and treason is called by the Holy Spirit faith and fear of God. This faith and fear of God was the reason why the work of Rahab was pleasing to God, and also her person, though previously she had been a woman of debauchery. And her work was not so perfect that it did not have sin on her part, and many weaknesses, which God bore with in His mercy, just as He bore with those of the midwives in Egypt who preferred to obey God rather than Pharaoh, as was already explained.

Now Rahab was not only praised in the Holy Scriptures

for having given aid and succor to the people of God against the duty and oath she owed to her country and nation according to men, and for having renounced these to make a covenant with the children of Israel, but was also adopted into the people of God, no more nor less than if she and her family had been born in the midst of the church of Israel and were of the very lineage and blood of Abraham and the other patriarchs (Josh. 2:12-17; 6:25). And therefore God showed her this grace, that she did not perish, and was not slain in the taking of Jericho as its other citizens and inhabitants, who were more loyal to their ruler and to their country and nation than she was (if the loyalty of the two is judged according to human understanding). Also, out of love for her, God made her family and friends partakers of this same mercy, who chose to follow and join in the covenant she had made with the Israelites. Furthermore, she was so advanced in honor among the people of God that she is numbered among the great mothers of this great king and prophet David, and she enjoyed a truly honored place in the genealogy of Jesus Christ (Matt. 1:5).

By this God has declared who those are who are most pleasing to Him, either those who are united and joined together, and who keep their oath toward each other in resisting the people of God and taking counsel together against them; or she who forsakes and abandons them to join herself with the people who she knows to be the people of God, being in covenant with Him. Therefore she had no qualms in revealing all that was passing in the city and in all the country against the Israelites, as much as she knew. Thus we see here the reversal of all the counsels of men and all their schemes.

Thus, seeing that it is so, we must not think that it is loyalty and fidelity to remain united with the wicked, with those to whom we are joined either by consanguinity or other alliances, when they join together against God. But we must consider this a revolution against God, and treason against

His Church and His people, if we give aid and favor to those united against the children of God. For there is neither faith nor loyalty in breaking the faith and loyalty we owe to God and His Church. For just as He cannot be separated from His Church, so also no one can be attached to her if he is not also attached to Him. Thus we ought not to be taken as disloyal or as traitors and betrayers when we separate ourselves from the wicked and their wicked cause in order to join ourselves to the righteous and God's cause. But we are disloyal, traitors, and betrayers if we keep the faith with the enemies of God by joining with them against Him and His servants.

We have another example to this purpose in Jonathan the son of Saul, which is even more suitable to the matter at hand than any of the others we have still to deal with. For the first, before Saul began to hate David and to persecute him as he later persecuted him, Jonathan displayed a great friendship for David, whom he loved as his own soul and life (1 Sam. 18:1). And therefore he made a covenant with David, with promises and vows, that they would never betray each other, but that their friendship and covenant would be perpetual, not only between them in their lifetime, but also between their successors after their death. Since Saul declared himself David's mortal enemy and bent all his efforts against him to put him to death as a traitor and enemy of the king his lord, yet Jonathan did not desist from the friendship he previously bore to David, but indeed increased it even greater (1 Sam. 19:1-2). Similarly he did not break the covenant he had made with him, but to the contrary he renewed and reconfirmed it many times after that, even during the time when Saul his father displayed his greatest rage and fury in pursuing David to death (1 Sam. 20:30-34; 23:16-18).

Now this friendship and covenant was not only made with words and a nice appearance, but also in truth. For Jonathan not only never united with Saul his father to aid him in pursuing David when he pursued him, but what is even more, he aided David in every way he could to deliver him from the traps and from the hands of Saul his father. For the first, he made a very strong remonstrance to his father of the injury which he did to David, and labored by every means possible to reconcile David to him and to restore him into his good favor (1 Sam. 19:1-7). We can judge the faith, conscience, and affection of Jonathan by what happened. For though Saul conceived a mortal hatred against David and was so transported with rage and fury by the evil spirit which drove him to this, nevertheless Jonathan took advantage of this blow, and slightly appeased this fury and rage of Saul, and reconciled him to David, and made Saul acknowledge the wrong he did to David his loyal and faithful servant.

On this let us firstly note the danger in which Jonathan placed himself by pursuing this reconciliation (1 Sam. 22:7-8). We can judge this by what Saul did to him immediately afterward. For Saul, becoming aware that Jonathan followed David's side and that he showed him all the favors that he could, was not content to complain about his son Jonathan to his servants and all those of his court and of his lineage of Benjamin, but also strongly reproached him to his face, greatly insulting him and accusing him of being a disobedient and traitorous son to his own father and king, whose heir he ought to be (1 Sam. 20:30-34). And what is even worse, he so forgot himself and so emptied himself of every fatherly affection and all humanity against his own son, that he deliberately sought to run him through with his spear and kill him, just as he had thought to kill David in this same way.

Yet all this did not prevent Jonathan from always keeping the faith and loyalty he had promised to David. And therefore Jonathan counseled with David in order to see how he could understand and know what desire Saul had toward David, and what hope of reconciliation he might have. They also counseled together on the means and signs by which Jonathan could make Saul's plots known to David, and what assurance or danger might be hanging over him, in order that he could guard himself from falling into Saul's hands.

If the cause of Saul and Jonathan were placed in judgment before the wise men of this world, what sentence would they pronounce? Doubtless they would judge that the complaint and accusation Saul made against Jonathan was most just and very reasonable, and that Jonathan was condemned in his cause. For to whom was Jonathan more obligated, to Saul his father and the king of Israel, or to David his brother-in-law, who was no more than a soldier and servant of the king? No matter what obligation he had to David because of the covenant he had made with him, it seems that he had a much greater one to Saul, and particularly for two reasons.

First, because Saul was his father, to whom he owed the honor and obedience that all children owe to their fathers and mothers by God's command (Ex. 20:12; Deut. 5:16; Eph. 6:1).

Second, because he was the king of Israel, who had been ordained by God.

Therefore even if Jonathan had not been his son, yet he owed him the homage and fidelity that all subjects by right owe their natural and lawful rulers. Thus did he not have sufficient reasons to break his covenant with David, and to join himself with Saul his father against him, seeing that David was declared by the king himself to be an enemy of the king? But far from Jonathan doing this, instead of breaking his friendship and covenant with him, he confirmed it ever more and more, as was already said (1 Sam. 19:1-7; 20:1-42; 23:16-18).

Thus shall we say that Jonathan was a rebellious and disobedient child who betrayed his own father and kingdom? We could rightly say this if he had risen up against Saul as Absalom rose up against David his father, to cast him out of his kingdom in order that he might reign himself in his father's stead (2 Sam. 15:1-12). But Jonathan did not have such a wicked heart. He never refused to obey Saul as his father and king in all the affairs of his house and of the kingdom whenever he could do so in accordance with God's commands. The wrongs and injuries Saul showered upon him did not turn him away from doing his duty and always faithfully acquitting himself of his office toward his father, both in feats of arms and all other things that served firstly to the honor of God and then to the honor and profit of Saul and his kingdom, and of all the people of God. In such a case he did not even spare his own life, as we have many certain testimonies of by his prowess and his own deeds (1 Sam. 18:1-15). In short, it did indeed happen that he lost his own life, not as Absalom in pursuing his own father, but as a valiant soldier and virtuous captain, battling alongside his father in the defense of his country and the people of God.

Therefore Jonathan cannot be accused of having failed in anything, either toward his father or toward his kingdom. But if he had done otherwise, he would have sinned greatly against God. For firstly, he would have set himself against God in the person of David His servant, as Saul had done. For what reason had Saul to persecute David? Jonathan knew quite well that Saul had no servant in all his court as faithful as David, and that he had no man in all his kingdom who could be—I do not even say preferred, but even compared with David in all things, as Jonathan truly declared to his father (1 Sam. 19:4-5). Also God gave this grace to Jonathan, that he truly recognized that David must reign by the ordinance of God, and that David's cause was very just (1 Sam. 23:16-17). Therefore he did not desire to resist the will of God and battle against Him as Saul his father had done with such rage and fury. For he knew that in doing this, not only would it profit him nothing, but also it would ever more and more provoke God's wrath against his father's house as well as against himself and all his posterity.

Furthermore, he recognized that the only reason Saul his father was inflamed against David was because of the envy he bore him, and because his mind was greatly troubled because he feared that the kingdom would be given to David, and that it would be transferred from the house of Saul to the house of David. In this Saul tormented himself without cause. For he was truly assured that David was not of so wicked a heart as to even think of working any evil against Saul, whom he had always honored, protected, and supported, no matter what wrong Saul did him. David had often shown him by personal experience that he had no desire to do him harm, seeing that Saul would have been killed many times over if David had wished to kill him, or even if he had only permitted others to have slain him (1 Sam. 24:4-10; 26:5-11). Thus Saul had no reason to fear that David was plotting any treason against him. But if it pleased the Lord to choose David instead of Saul, Saul labored in vain if he thought to hinder the counsel of God. For he strove against God, and not against David.

Jonathan indeed considered all these things well. Therefore he is shown to be much better and wiser than Saul his father. For he was also led by another spirit, and feared God more than he feared his father.

If Jonathan had done otherwise, not only would he have taken up arms against God and done great wrong to David (as Saul did), but he would also have poorly rendered his duty to his father. For what greater good could he have done him than to strive to hinder him from fighting against God and harming His servants, and staining his hands with the blood of innocent men? How could he better show himself more loyal, both to his father and to all the kingdom, than to be engaged in breaking the evil schemes of his father and of all the flatterers who were in his court, by which he saw that Saul would destroy his own house and his own kingdom, with all the people of God? For who better procured the honor and profit of Saul and all the kingdom: Jonathan and the other servants of Saul who gave him good and faithful counsel to be reconciled with David, or the envious, flatterers, and false witnesses who like firebrands incited Saul as much as they could to persecute God's people? Who are those to whom the Word of God gives more praise, and who is it that receives the greater condemnation in this matter?

CHAPTER ELEVEN

A Christian's Duty Under Ungodly Rulers

In the following excerpt Viret addresses the duty of believers in times of oppression and tribulation. Drawing from the examples of Jeremiah, Esther, and others like them, he declares that whenever Christians find themselves in a situation similar to that of the children of Israel in Egypt, the reign of ungodly kings in Israel and Judah, or the Babylonian captivity, they must follow the counsel given them by the prophets of God in those times of captivity and persecution.

Let us consider what these people of God did. Jeremiah did not tell the people that they ought to rebel, and disturb and violate the faith that the king had given to Nebuchadnezzar and to the Babylonians. To the contrary, he admonishes all alike to obey them, and to remain faithful and loyal to them as to their own sovereign rulers, and to pay the tributes they required. And he promised them that if they did this, it would turn out well for them in the end (Jer. 29:7). But if they did the opposite, they would offend God, who willed for them to be subject to the Babylonians because of their sins. Therefore they must take it as assured that evil would come upon them and that they would be even more greatly oppressed and subjected if they did not follow what the Lord commanded them by His prophet.

The false prophets of that day preached completely the opposite. They gave the people who still remained in Judah the boldness and impudence to rebel against the Babylonians their lords, whom God had given them in order to chastise them (Jer. 27:14; 28:1-4). These false prophets promised victory and all prosperity if the people would only follow their counsel. And because these prophets spoke more to the liking and according to the desires of the king, his court, and the people, their counsel was believed instead of Jeremiah's. But what happened in the end? Exactly what Jeremiah had predicted. For he had the word of God; but the others did not. They followed their own spirit only, and not the Spirit of God. Thus they received their own wages (Jer. 39:6-7).

Now in the eyes of the people of Israel at that time, the Babylonians were regarded nearly as the Turks are today in the eyes of Christians. If God thus willed for His people to obey the Babylonians until the time He had determined for their captivity was expired, we must not doubt that He requires as much of us when we are under tyrant rulers, and even more when they bear the name of Christians, and there is greater hope of being able to win them to Jesus Christ than the Turks.

Thus we must follow the example of the Israelites and the saints whom we mentioned previously. We must have recourse to tears, fasts, prayers, and supplications, and must humble ourselves before God with true repentance, being assured that God will deliver us. But if we desire Him to deliver us, we must first remove the cause of the indignation He has against us, which is the reason of our captivity.

Seeing that our sins are the cause of all our evil, we must not seek a remedy among the creatures, or it will happen to us as it did to the woman with the issue of blood. We will spend all our livelihood on physicians, and our sickness will only grow worse until we address ourselves to Jesus (Luke 8:43). It is He who will pardon our sins and afterward deliver us from the bonds and scourges of Satan and the antichrist.

If we wish to find Jesus, we must seek Him. To seek Him well, we must seek Him in true repentance, in genuine fear of God, with true confession of our sins. We must not do as many have done, and still do. We must not excuse ourselves, and seek to cover our sins by excuses and false appearances in an attempt to justify ourselves before men. For it will do us precious little good to appear justified before men if we are not so before God. Now we cannot be so before God except by means of Jesus Christ (Rom. 3:21-22; 4:23-25). And Jesus Christ did not come for the just, but for sinners; not for the healthy, but for the sick (Matt. 9:12-13). Thus if we wish to be justified and healed by Him, it is necessary for us to confess that we are sinners and sick.

We are not more just than Daniel, Ezra, Nehemiah, Mordecai, and Esther (Dan. 9:3-19). Thus we have no more shame in humbling ourselves before God and confessing our iniquities and sins, and those of our kings, rulers, and fathers, than these had who did the same. For this is the counsel that Moses gave to the people, and the remedy he taught for their deliverance from captivity. He says, "If they shall confess their iniquity, and the iniquity of their fathers, with their trespass which they trespassed against Me, and that also they have walked contrary unto Me; and that I also have walked contrary unto them, and have brought them into the land of their enemies; if then their uncircumcised hearts be humbled, and they then accept of the punishment of their iniquity: then will I remember My covenant with Jacob, and also My covenant with Isaac, and also My covenant with Abraham will I remember; and I will remember the land" (Lev. 26:40-42; Deut. 30:1-10). He does not counsel them to take up any arms except those of repentance, faith, fasts, prayers, and supplications.

But how do we act now? How do many—indeed, the vast majority—of those who boast of the Gospel live? They are often the most dissolute of all. They follow the lifestyles of the Papists, idolaters, and earthly and carnal men, without repentance, without amendment of life, without giving any good example, either by their life or conversation. They are often the first at dances, plays, taverns, brothels, and other houses of dissolution. In short, there is no way of telling them apart from unbelievers.

Neither Mordecai, nor the Jews that were with him, nor Esther, nor her damsels at court acted in such a way when they saw the hand of God extended over them, and the fury of their enemies armed against them. So also they did not despair, but appealed to the Lord. And we, for lack of doing like them, have not obtained what they obtained. For we too often trust in the assistance of men. We are too slothful and lazy to return to God. And if we do return, it is not with such a heart and such faith as God requires. We experience what James says, "Ye have not, because ye ask not. Ye ask, and receive not, because ye ask amiss, that ye may consume it upon your lusts" (James 4:2-3).

Thus it is firstly required that we pray. But it is not enough to simply pray. We must pray as we ought, and in such a way that God is not more dishonored by our prayers than if we had not prayed at all.

Thus let us all hasten to take up these arms—that is, tears, cries, sighs, and groans, and fasts, prayers, and supplications, with a true change of life. And when God has sufficiently humbled us, and when we acknowledge our sins, we will hear Him speak to us as He spoke in the time of Moses, "I have surely seen the affliction of My people which are in Egypt, and have heard their cry, . . . and I am come down to deliver them" (Ex. 3:7-8). He will send us servants and captains to deliver us by His strong and stretched out arm (Ex. 6:6). He will command Pharaoh to let His people go, that they might serve Him. And if Pharaoh does not, but instead hardens his heart, God will send such plagues upon him and all his people that they will be utterly cast down and destroyed, as He did previously with the Egyptians and their king.

Thus let us wait upon the Lord. Let us wait for the assistance He has prepared, and let us not be led astray by our own whims or imaginations. Let us wait for the time that He has ordained. For just as He defined the time of the captivity of the children of Israel in Egypt and Babylon, so also He has determined our time, which we can neither hasten nor delay any more than the day of our death (Job 14:5). Let us therefore wait with all patience. For God wills to wholly deliver us as soon as He has humbled us and proved and mortified us by the cross, seeing that He knows what is for our good.

God did not immediately give Abraham, his seed, or his descendants the land of Canaan which He had promised them. And how long did He lead Joseph before the fulfillment of his dreams and before he was exalted to the glory and dignity He had prepared for him? The poor paralytic who was waiting to be healed at the pool of Bethesda in Jerusalem, did he not remain sick thirty-eight years before he was healed by Jesus Christ? (John 5:5). And what of the lame man whom Peter healed, and Aeneas the paralytic also? Did they not wait a very long time in terrible misery from both their diseases? For Aeneas remained so eight years (Acts 3:2; 9:33). And the lame man was lame from his mother's womb, without being able to care for himself more than forty years, before he was healed. And how long did the Canaanite woman cry after Jesus Christ before He paid any attention to her? (Matt. 15:22-28).

Yet every one of these people obtained comfort in the end, and received more blessings from God than they could ever have imagined. And the poor blind man whom John wrote about, why wasn't he healed earlier? They all had to wait for the time ordained of God, in which He willed to be glorified in them (John 9:3).

Therefore let us wait upon the Lord with all patience, and with true hope. And then we will experience what

Jeremiah declares that He has promised to His people: "And I will be found of you, saith the Lord: and I will turn away your captivity, and I will gather you from all the nations, and from all the places whither I have driven you, saith the Lord; and I will bring you again into the place whence I caused you to be carried away captive" (Jer. 29:14). "For it shall come to pass in that day, saith the Lord of hosts, that I will break his yoke from off thy neck, and will burst thy bonds, and strangers shall no more serve themselves of him" (Jer. 30:8).

Thus let us say with David, "though I walk through the valley of the shadow of death, I will fear no evil: for Thou art with me" (Ps. 23:4). He left Lazarus, the brother of Mary and Martha, without assistance for so long that he remained in the grave four days, so that he already stank (John 11:39). Yet He did not abandon him at all, but gave him aid even in death in order to teach us that He will be our aid, no matter how slowly He comes. Indeed, even in death He will aid us, for He is stronger than death (1 Sam. 2:6).

A Note on Sources

The excerpts for this work have been taken from the following writings of Pierre Viret:

Chapter One: "How Should Man be Governed?"

    Text is taken from Viret's introduction to his commentary on the Ten Commandments, published under the title *Instruction Chrestienne en la doctrine de la loi et de l'Evangile* (Geneva: Jean Rivery, 1564), pages 249-256.

Chapter Two: "Warning Against Insurrection and Rebellion"

    The text of Viret's letter is translated from a collection of letters he published in 1559 under the title *Epistres aus Fideles, pour les instruire et les admonester et exhorter touchant leur office, et pour les consoler en leurs tribulations* (Geneva: Jean Rivery), pages 205-217.

Chapter Three: "Christians the Best of Subjects"

    Text is taken from a collection of several of Viret's writings published under the title *Traittez divers pour l'instruction des fideles qui resident & conversent és lieus & pais esquels il ne leur est permis de vivre en la pureté & liberté de l'Evangile* (Geneva: Jean Rivery, 1559). This excerpt is translated from the final title in that volume: *Remonstrances aus fideles qui conversent entre les papists,* pages 115-119.

Chapter Four: "Honoring Those in Authority Over Us"

    Text is taken from Viret's commentary on the Ten Commandments, published under the title *Instruction Chrestienne en la doctrine de la loi et de l'Evangile* (Geneva: Jean Rivery, 1564), pages 449-458. This excerpt is translated from his commentary on the fifth commandment.

Chapter Five: "The Ministry of the Magistrates"

    Text is a record of Viret's address given at the Lausanne Disputation of 1536. The text is taken from *Les Actes de la Dispute de Lausanne 1536* (Secrétariat de l'Université: Neuchatel, 1928), pages 298-304.

Chapter Six: "The Magistrate's Role Under God"

    Text is taken from Viret's work *Instruction Chrestienne en la doctrine de la loi et de l'Evangile* (Geneva: Jean Rivery, 1564), pages 122-125.

Chapter Seven: "Jurisdictions, Offices, and Callings Ordained by God"

    Text is taken from Viret's *Traittez divers pour l'instruction des fideles.* This excerpt is translated from the final title in that volume: *Remonstrances aus fideles qui conversent entre les papists,* pages 24-41 and 201-202.

A Note on Sources

Chapter Eight: "Using the Magistrate for Good"

    Text is taken from Viret's *Remonstrances aus fideles*, pages 268-276.

Chapter Nine: "When Can Christians Wage War?"

    Text is taken from Viret's *Remonstrances aus fideles*, pages 282-299.

Chapter Ten: "True Obedience to Magistrates: Examples from Scripture"

    Text is taken from Viret's *Remonstrances aus fideles*, pages 299-317.

Chapter Eleven: "A Christian's Duty Under Ungodly Rulers"

    Text is taken from Viret's *Remonstrances aus fideles*, pages 209-217.

Letters of Comfort
to the Persecuted Church

by Pierre Viret
translated by R. A. Sheats

Softcover, 114 pages
ISBN: 978-1-938822-50-6

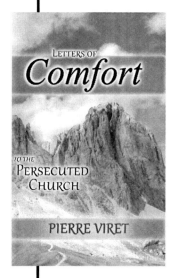

From the depths of a pastor's heart come letters of hearty biblical comfort for persecuted believers. Written to men and women facing imprisonment, banishment, suffering, and death, these letters capture the heart of the Gospel and offer consolation and sincere comfort for those suffering for the sake of Christ.

Written by Pierre Viret (1511-1571), a Swiss Reformer and close friend of John Calvin, these letters overflow with a pastoral concern for the souls as well as the physical needs of his readers. Republished several times throughout the Reformation era, Viret's letters appear now for the first time in the English language, and the comfort they offer to an afflicted church is as pertinent today as it was the day he wrote them.

PIERRE VIRET:
The Angel of the Reformation

by R. A. Sheats

Hardcover, 323 pages
ISBN: 978-098437817

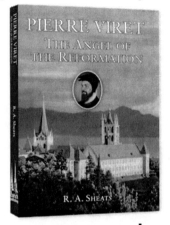

For the first time in five hundred years, a full biography of Pierre Viret is now available to the English-speaking world. Packed with fascinating details and bristling with original documents and letters of the Reformers, the history of this forgotten giant of the Reformation is recounted in an interesting and enthralling way. Known by his contemporaries as *the Angel of the Reformation*, Viret was truly a radiant light amongst the men of his generation, a light which has finally been uncovered in this our day. May the unveiling of this precious life inspire and equip a new generation of Reformers as they seek to extend God's glory to every area of human existence!

"R. A. has written a superb biography on our Swiss Reformer that is both warmhearted and scholarly. We anticipate a soon translation into French."

- **Daniel Bovet**, President of *l'Association Pierre Viret*, Switzerland

CPSIA information can be obtained at www.ICGtesting.com
Printed in the USA
LVOW06s0151280715

447794LV00003B/6/P